Big Book of Things to Do

Ray Gibson

Edited by Fiona Watt and Felicity Everett
Designed by Amanda Barlow
Illustrated by Sue Stitt, Mikki Rain, Kim Lane,
Michaela Kennard and Chris Chaisty
Photographs by Howard Allman and Ray Moller
Food stylist: Ricky Turner • Face painter: Caro Childs
Series editor: Jenny Tyler

Contents

What shall I cook?

Contents

Before you start any of the recipes in this book, make sure that you have
all the things you will need. Always ask someone to help you to switch
on your oven to the correct temperature, before you begin to cook.
Also ask for help when you put things into an oven or take things out of
it. Wear a pair of oven mitts before you pick up
anything which might be hot.

Chocolate octopuses

For ten octopuses, you will need:
$2/3$ cup soft margarine
$2/3$ cup sugar
1 medium egg
3 teaspoons cocoa powder
$1^1/3$ cups flour
candy for eyes
greased cookie sheet

For butter icing:
3 tablespoons butter
$1/2$ cup powdered sugar

1. Mix the sugar and margarine in a bowl with a wooden spoon until they are creamy.

2. Sift the flour and the cocoa into the bowl. Add the egg and mix them well to make dough.

3. Use your hands to press the dough into a large ball. Wrap it in plastic food wrap.

4. Put the wrapped dough into a freezer for 30 minutes or into a refrigerator for an hour.

Heat the oven to 375°F

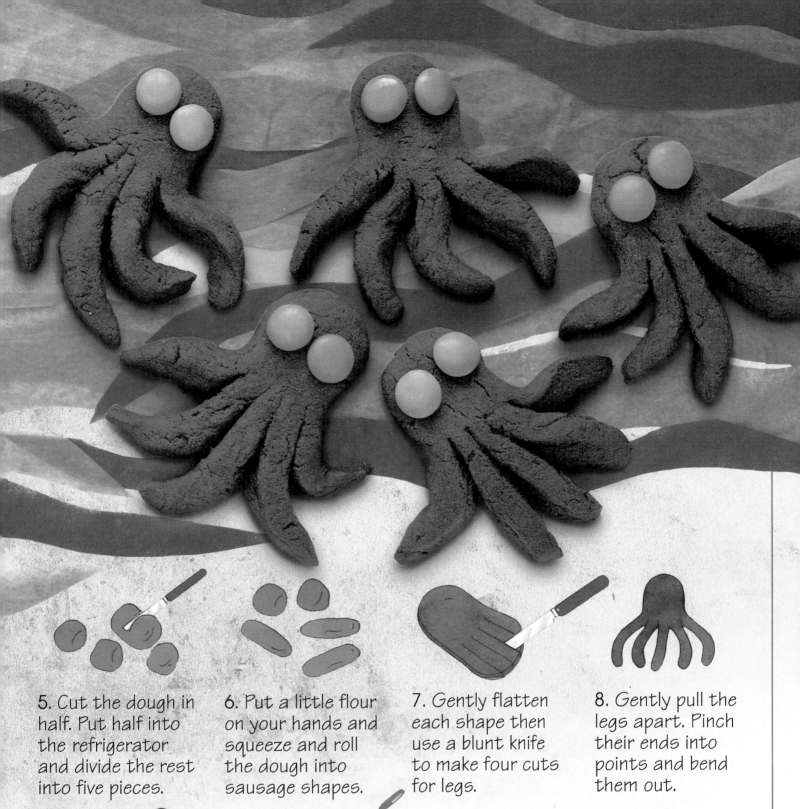

5. Cut the dough in half. Put half into the refrigerator and divide the rest into five pieces.

6. Put a little flour on your hands and squeeze and roll the dough into sausage shapes.

7. Gently flatten each shape then use a blunt knife to make four cuts for legs.

8. Gently pull the legs apart. Pinch their ends into points and bend them out.

9. Take the other half of dough out of the refrigerator and make five more octopuses.

10. Lift the octopuses onto a cookie sheet. Bake them for 10-12 minutes.

11. Leave them to cool for a little while before putting them on a cooling rack.

12. Follow step 7 on page 21 to make icing. Put some icing on the candy. Press them on for eyes.

Jam tarts

For about 12 tarts, you will need:
¾ cup of flour
2 tablespoons softened margarine
2 tablespoons shortening
2 tablespoons of very cold water
pinch of salt
½ cup of jam or preserves
greased mini-muffin pans
round cookie cutter
tiny cookie cutters

Making pastry

To make the tarts

1. Rub the flour, salt, margarine and shortening so that it looks like crumbs.

2. Add the water. Use a blunt knife to mix it in. Squeeze it into a ball of dough.

3. Sprinkle flour onto your work surface. Roll the dough to ⅛in thick.

4. Press out 12 shapes from the dough with the round cutter.

If you don't have any tiny cutters use a bottle top instead.

Heat the oven to 400°F

5. Push the shapes into a greased pan. Put two teaspoons of jam into each one.

6. Press out some shapes with the tiny cutters. Put one on each tart.

7. Bake the tarts for about 15 minutes in your oven.

8. Be careful, as the tarts will be very hot. Leave them to cool on a rack.

Wait until the tarts are cold to eat them.

Cheesy snakes and caterpillars

For about eight snakes and four caterpillars, you will need:
1¼ cups self-rising flour
½ teaspoon salt
¼ cup margarine
²/₃ cup cheese, finely grated
1 egg and 2 tablespoons milk, beaten together
raisins for eyes
a bottle top
greased cookie sheet

1. Sift the flour and salt. Add the margarine and rub it with your fingers to make crumbs.

2. Leave a tablespoon of cheese on a saucer. Add the rest to the bowl and stir it in.

3. Put a tablespoon of the egg mixture in a cup. Mix the rest into the flour to make dough.

4. Roll out the dough on a floury surface, until it is as thick as your little finger.

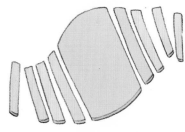
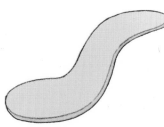
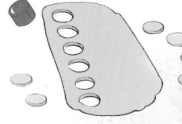

5. Use a blunt knife to cut eight strips as wide as two of your fingers.

6. Bend the strips into wiggles. Pinch the ends. Press one end flat for a head.

7. To make a caterpillar, cut out six circles of dough with a bottle top.

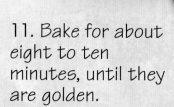

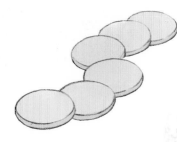

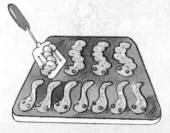

8. Lay the circles in a line. Overlap the edges and press them together.

9. Brush the shapes with the egg mixture. Sprinkle with cheese. Add raisins for eyes.

10. Use a spatula to lift the shapes onto a greased cookie sheet.

11. Bake for about eight to ten minutes, until they are golden.

     Heat the oven to 400°F

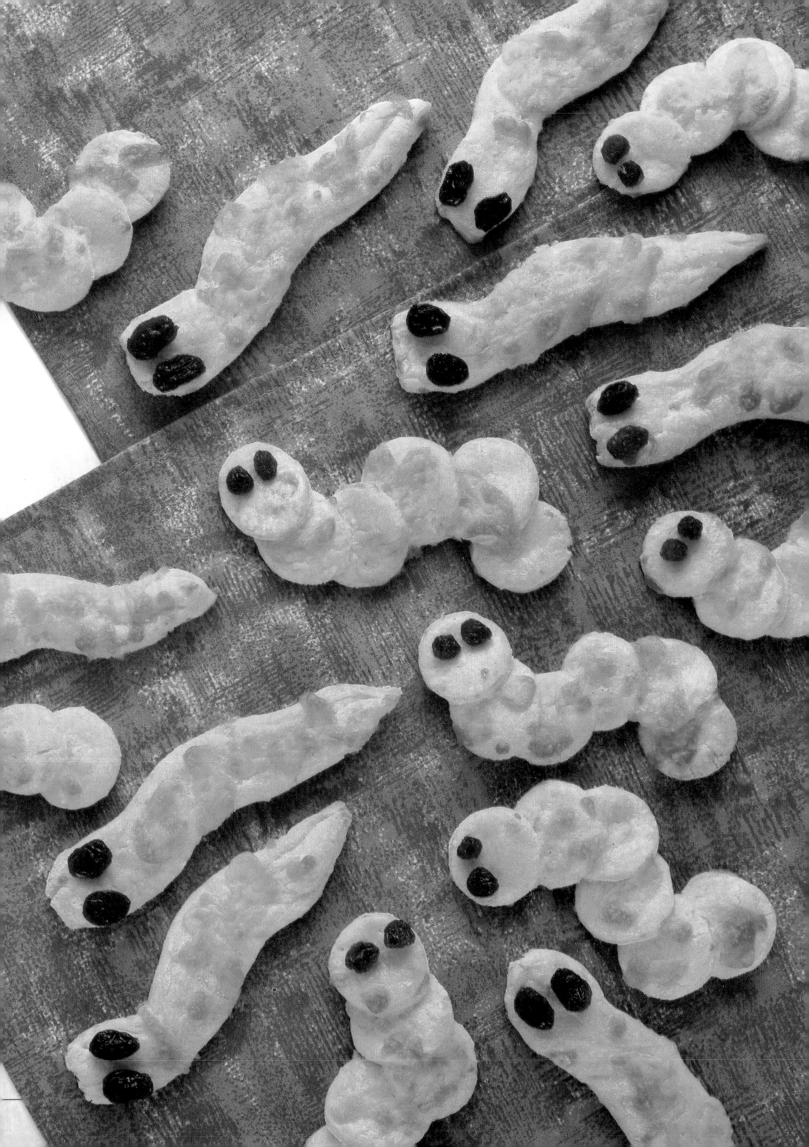

Owl cakes

For ten owls, you will need:
$1^2/_3$ cups whole-wheat flour
1 teaspoon ground cinnamon
2 level teaspoons baking powder
$^1/_3$ cup margarine
½ cup brown sugar
1 medium-sized cooking apple, chopped finely
1 egg, beaten
10 maraschino cherries, chopped in half
10 shelled whole almonds
raisins
greased cookie sheet

1. Mix the flour, cinnamon and baking powder together in a bowl.

2. Cut the margarine into lumps. Add it to the bowl. Rub it in with your fingers.

3. When the mixture looks like crumbs mix in the sugar, apple and egg.

These owls are delicious if you eat them warm with ice cream.

4. Lift out a heaped tablespoon of the mixture. Put it on a cookie sheet.

5. Squeeze the mixture to make a body shape. Make nine more owls.

6. For eyes, press in two cherry pieces. Add an almond for a beak.

7. Bake the owls for about 15 minutes, until they are golden brown.

8. Let the owls cool for a few minutes then put them on a rack.

9. When the owls are cool, press a raisin into the middle of each eye.

Upside-down cake

This cake is made upside-down with the topping at the bottom of the dish. You turn it over once it has cooked.
For the cake, you will need
1 cup self-rising flour
2 eggs
⅓ cup sugar
3 tablespoon soft margarine

For the topping, you will need:
2 tablespoon butter
14½oz. can of apricot halves, drained
maraschino cherries
½ cup brown sugar

8in. ovenproof cake pan

For the cake:

1. Sift the flour into a big bowl. Add the eggs, margarine and sugar to the bowl.

2. Stir everything together with a wooden spoon until you get a smooth creamy mixture.

For the topping:

3. Grease the sides of a cake pan. Melt the butter. Pour it all over the bottom.

4. Use your fingers to sprinkle the brown sugar evenly on top of the butter.

5. Put the apricots around the edge, cut-side up. Fill in the middle. Put cherries in the gaps.

6. Spread the cake batter over the fruit. Bake on the middle rack for 45 minutes.

Ice cream goes well with this cake.

7. Loosen the edges with a knife. Turn the cake upside-down onto a big plate.

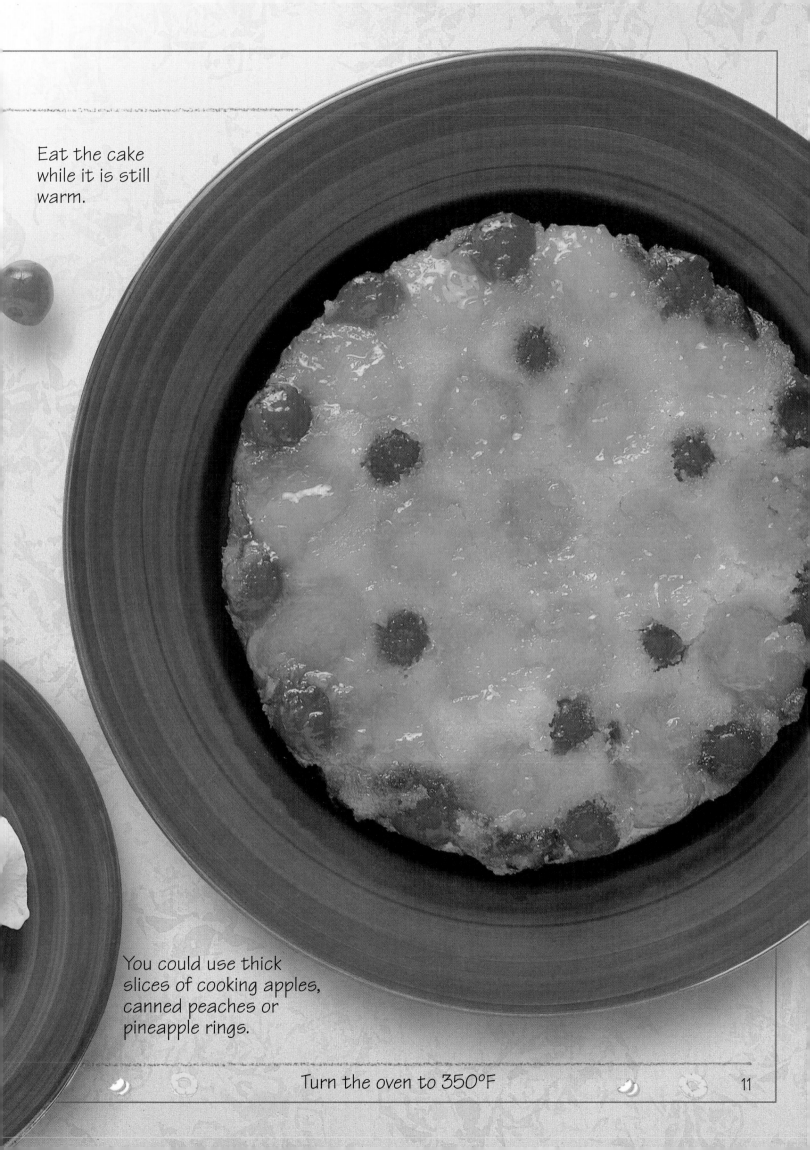

Eat the cake
while it is still
warm.

You could use thick
slices of cooking apples,
canned peaches or
pineapple rings.

Shining star cookies

For about 24 cookies, you will need:
½ cup soft brown sugar
⅓ cup soft margarine
half a small beaten egg
1¼ cups flour
1 teaspoon allspice
hard candy, assorted flavors
a greased cookie sheet
large star-shaped cookie cutter
small round cookie cutter, slightly bigger than the candy
fat drinking straw

You can use any shape of hard candy.

1. Mix the sugar and margarine really well, getting rid of any lumps.

2. Mix in half of the beaten egg, a little at a time. You don't need the other half.

3. Sift in the flour and the spice. Mix it really well with a blunt knife.

4. Squeeze the mixture together with your hands to make a firm dough.

5. Roll out the dough on a floury surface until it is ¼in. thick.

6. Press out star shapes. Lift them carefully onto the cookie sheet.

7. Make a hole in each star by pressing the straw in one of the points.

8. Use a small cookie cutter to cut out a shape in the middle of each star.

   Heat the oven to 350ºF

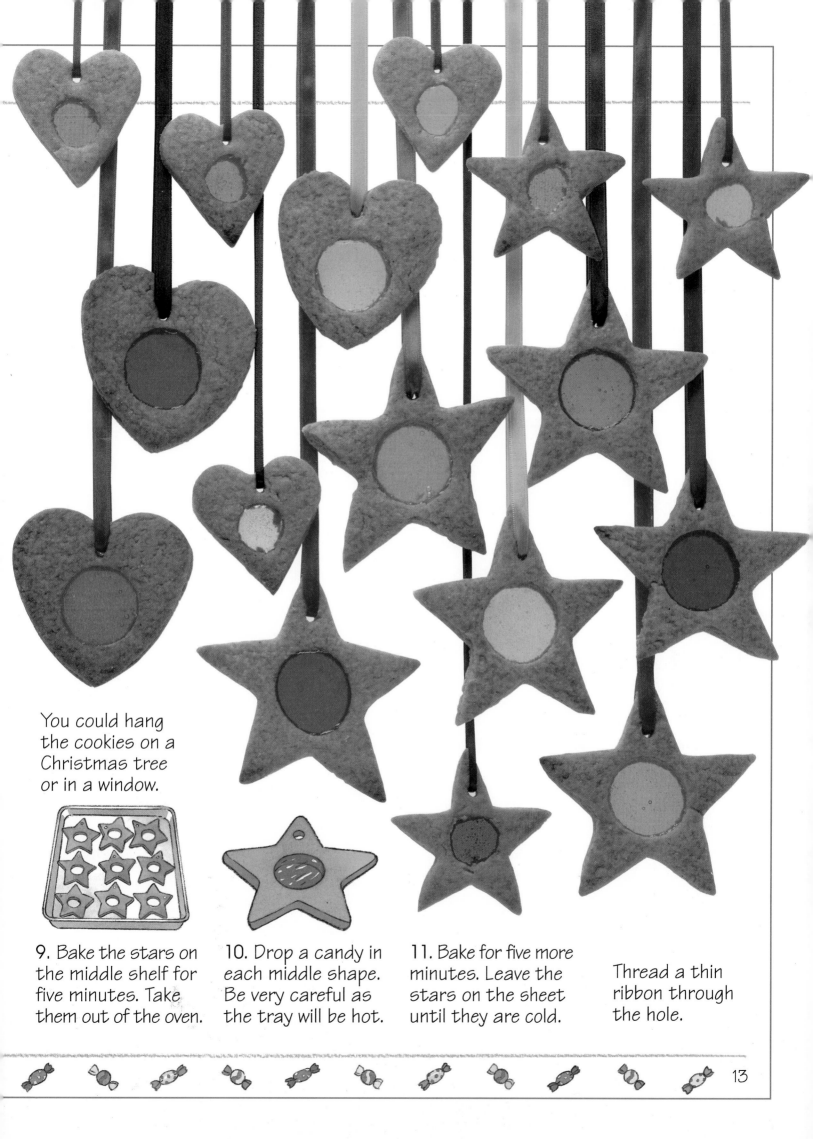

You could hang the cookies on a Christmas tree or in a window.

9. Bake the stars on the middle shelf for five minutes. Take them out of the oven.

10. Drop a candy in each middle shape. Be very careful as the tray will be hot.

11. Bake for five more minutes. Leave the stars on the sheet until they are cold.

Thread a thin ribbon through the hole.

Apricot muffins

For 9 muffins, you will need:
1 cup self-rising flour
1/2 cup whole-wheat flour
1 teaspoon of baking powder
1 teaspoon of allspice
2/3 cup dried apricots, chopped
7/8 cup of milk
1/4 cup melted butter
1 egg
2 teaspoons of lemon juice
2/3 cup packed brown sugar
greased muffin pan

1. Sift the self-rising flour. Add the whole-wheat flour and baking powder.

2. Add the spice and apricots. Use a big spoon to mix them in very well.

3. Beat the milk, butter, egg, lemon juice and sugar in another bowl.

4. Use a spoon to make a large hole in the middle of the flour mixture.

You could add maraschino cherries, instead of apricots.

5. Pour in half of the beaten mixture. Stir it well. Pour in the rest and mix gently.

6. Put some mix in each hole in the pan. Don't smooth the tops.

You can also make these muffins with chocolate chips, but leave out the spice.

7. Bake for about 20-25 minutes, until the tops are golden brown.

8. Leave the muffins in the pan for five minutes. Put them on a rack to cool.

Flower candy

You will need:
2 cups powdered sugar, sifted
half the white of a small egg, beaten
1 tablespoon lemon juice
¼ teaspoon peppermint flavoring
yellow and red food dyes
a cookie sheet covered in plastic foodwrap
small flower cookie cutter

1. Sift the powdered sugar into a bowl. Make a hole in the middle of it with a spoon.

2. In a small bowl, mix the egg white, lemon juice and the peppermint. Pour it into the sugar.

3. Use a blunt knife to stir the mixture. Then squeeze it between your fingers until it is smooth.

4. Cut the mixture into three pieces of the same size. Put each piece into a bowl.

5. Put a few drops of red food dye into one of the bowls. Use a metal spoon to mix it well.

6. Put a few drops of yellow food dye into one of the other bowls. Mix it in very well.

7. Sprinkle a little powdered sugar on a work surface. Roll the yellow mixture until it is this thick.

8. Use a cookie cutter to cut out as many flowers as you can, close together.

9. Use a blunt knife to lift the flowers onto a cookie sheet. Make red flowers in the same way.

10. Pull off a piece of white mixture about this size. Roll it in your hands to make a ball.

11. Press the ball to flatten it a little then press it into the middle of a flower shape.

12. Make lots more white balls and press them into the middles of the flowers.

13. Leave the flowers on the cookie sheet for at least an hour until they become hard.

Put some candy into a box for a present.

Hot bunnies

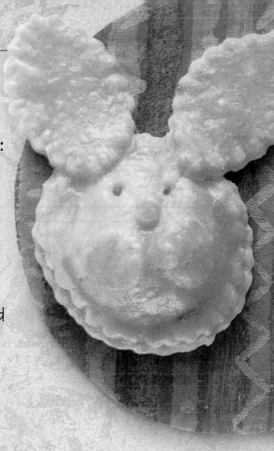

For four bunnies, you will need:

For the pastry:
1¼ cups flour
6 tablespoons margarine
6 teaspoons very cold water
pinch of salt

For the filling:
¼ cup sausage meat, browned
1 egg, beaten
large round cookie cutter
bottle top
fat straw
greased cookie sheet

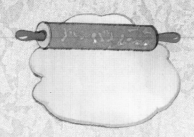

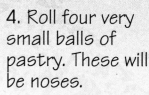

1. Make the pastry in a big bowl following steps 1 and 2 on page 4.

2. Sprinkle some flour onto a work surface. Roll out the pastry thinly.

3. Cut three circles with the cutter and two with the bottle top, for each rabbit.

4. Roll four very small balls of pastry. These will be noses.

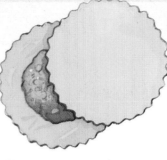

5. Use a pastry brush to paint one of the large circles with beaten egg.

6. Put a big teaspoon of sausage meat in the middle.

7. Lay one of the big circles on top and flatten it gently with your hand.

8. Press your finger all around the edge to join the circles.

   Heat the oven to 400°F

9. Brush the tops with egg. Lift them onto a cookie sheet with a spatula.

10. Press on two of the small bottle-top circles for cheeks. Add a nose.

11. Cut one ear by pressing the cutter halfway across one of the big circles.

12. Cut another ear from the other side of the circle.

13. Press the ears at the top. Brush the ears, nose and cheeks with egg.

14. Make two eyes by pushing the end of the straw into the pastry.

To make a pig, cut out the ears and nose with the bottle top. Cut nostrils with a straw.

15. Bake in the oven for about 15 minutes or until they are golden.

Crown cake

For the cake, you will need:
2/3 cup soft margarine
2/3 cup sugar
1 cup self-rising flour
2 eggs
8in. cake pan

For the decoration:
8 ice cream cones
ribbon
maraschino cherries
candy and cake decorations

For the butter icing:
½ cup soft butter
1½ cups powdered sugar
a few drops of lemon juice

To make the cake

1. Mix the sugar and margarine well until the mixture becomes creamy.

2. Beat one of the eggs and a little flour into the mixture.

3. Add the other egg and some more flour. Beat them in.

4. Gently mix in the rest of the flour with a metal spoon.

5. Grease the pan. Spoon the mixture in. Bake for about 40-45 minutes.

6. Leave for three to four minutes, then turn the cake out onto a cooling rack.

Decorating the cake

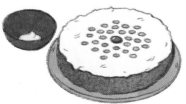

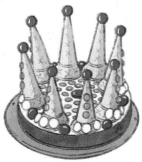

7. Make the icing by mixing the butter and powdered sugar. Add the lemon juice.

8. Put a tablespoon of icing in a bowl. Spread the rest on top. Decorate the middle with candy.

9. Pinch the ends off the cones. Press them on. Wrap some ribbon around the cake and tape it.

10. Dip the cherries in the spare icing. Press one on each cone. Add more cherries and candy.

Little cheese tarts

For about 12 tarts, you will need:
1¼ cups flour
6 tablespoons margarine
6 teaspoons very cold water
pinch of salt
small can of corn, drained
½ cup cheese, grated
1 egg
3 tablespoons milk
round cookie cutter
miniature aluminum pie pans

1. Make some pastry in a big bowl following steps 1 and 2 on page 4.

2. Sprinkle a little flour onto a work surface. Roll out the pastry thinly.

3. Cut out 12 circles with the cutter. Cut them close together.

4. Grease the pie pans. Press the circles gently into each pan.

5. Carefully put a heaped teaspoon of corn into each circle.

6. Sprinkle some grated cheese on top of the corn.

7. Beat the egg and the milk in a jug. Pour a little into each tart.

8. Bake them for 15-20 minutes until they are golden and puffy.

9. Lift the tarts onto a rack and leave them for a little while to cool.

You can eat the tarts when they are either warm or cold.

Heat the oven to 375 ºF

Painted cookies

To make about 20 cookies you will need:
½ cup powdered sugar, sifted
½ cup soft margarine
the yolk from a large egg
a few drops of vanilla extract
1¼ cups flour, sifted
cookie cutters
greased cookie sheet

To decorate the cookies:
beaten egg yolk
food dyes

1. Mix the powdered sugar and the margarine until they are smooth.

2. Mix in the egg yolk, stirring it well. Add a few drops of vanilla extract.

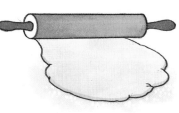

3. Hold a wire mesh strainer over the bowl and shake the flour through it.

4. Mix the flour in with a wooden spoon until you get a smooth dough.

5. Wrap the dough in food wrap. Put it in a freezer while you mix the dyes.

6. Put some egg yolk onto saucers. Mix a few drops of food dye with each.

7. Roll out half the dough quite thinly on a floury surface. Then roll the rest.

8. Use big cutters to press out shapes. Cut them close together.

9. Use a spatula to lift the cookies carefully onto a cookie sheet.

10. Press lightly with small cutters to make patterns on the cookies.

11. Use a very clean paintbrush to paint shapes with the dyes.

12. Bake them for 10-12 minutes. Let them cool a little. Put them on a rack.

Decorate your cookies with lots of different patterns.

This makes lots of cookies so you could freeze some of the dough to use another day.

Coconut mice

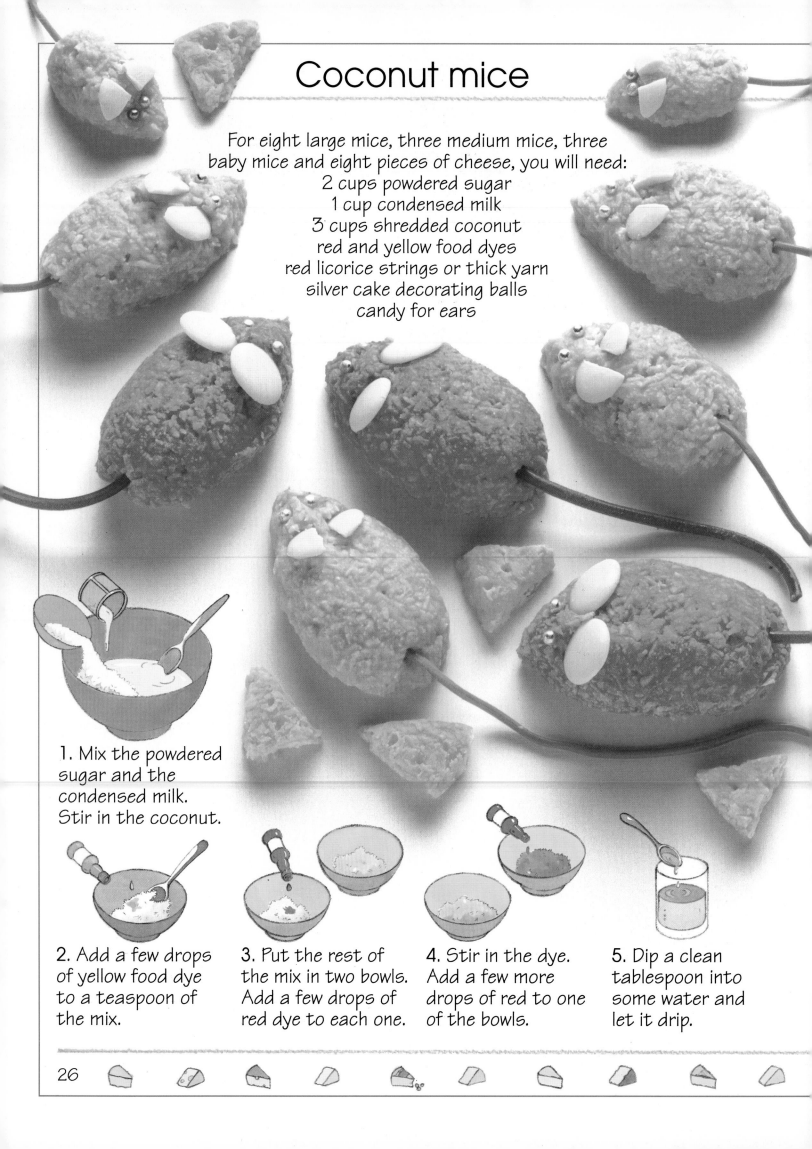

For eight large mice, three medium mice, three
baby mice and eight pieces of cheese, you will need:
2 cups powdered sugar
1 cup condensed milk
3 cups shredded coconut
red and yellow food dyes
red licorice strings or thick yarn
silver cake decorating balls
candy for ears

1. Mix the powdered
sugar and the
condensed milk.
Stir in the coconut.

2. Add a few drops
of yellow food dye
to a teaspoon of
the mix.

3. Put the rest of
the mix in two bowls.
Add a few drops of
red dye to each one.

4. Stir in the dye.
Add a few more
drops of red to one
of the bowls.

5. Dip a clean
tablespoon into
some water and
let it drip.

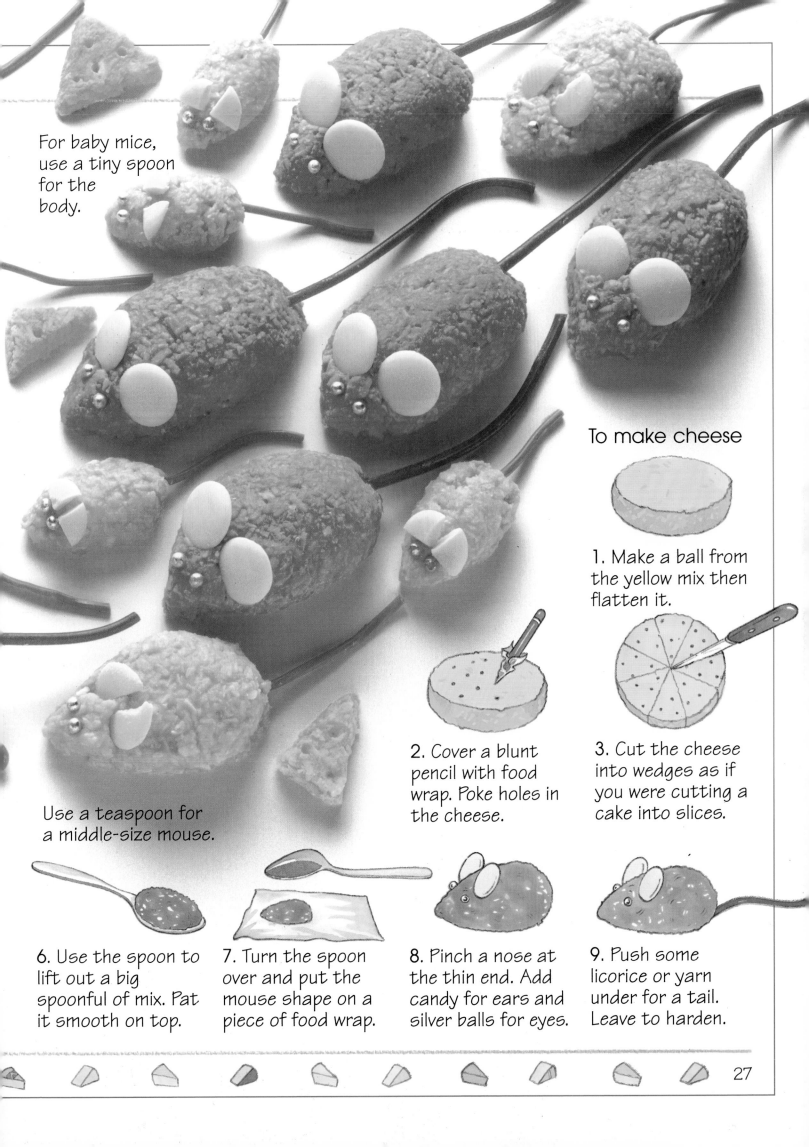

For baby mice, use a tiny spoon for the body.

Use a teaspoon for a middle-size mouse.

To make cheese

1. Make a ball from the yellow mix then flatten it.

2. Cover a blunt pencil with food wrap. Poke holes in the cheese.

3. Cut the cheese into wedges as if you were cutting a cake into slices.

6. Use the spoon to lift out a big spoonful of mix. Pat it smooth on top.

7. Turn the spoon over and put the mouse shape on a piece of food wrap.

8. Pinch a nose at the thin end. Add candy for ears and silver balls for eyes.

9. Push some licorice or yarn under for a tail. Leave to harden.

Easy pizza

Cheese and corn

For one 10in. pizza, you will need:
1¼ cups flour
½ teaspoon of salt
2 tablespoon oil
⅔ cup milk
⅔ cup cheese, grated
3 tomatoes, thinly sliced
mixed dried herbs

Topping ideas:
sliced mushrooms
corn
(canned or frozen)
pineapple
chopped ham
pepperoni

1. Sift the flour and salt together in a big bowl. Make a hole in the middle with a spoon.

2. Mix the milk with the oil in a jug. Mix it well. Pour it carefully into the hole in the flour.

Pepperoni, mushroom and cheese

28

3. Use a blunt knife to stir the mixture well, until it makes a sticky dough.

4. Sprinkle a little flour onto a work surface. Roll the dough into a circle as wide as this page.

6. Add more toppings if you want. Bake on the top rack for 15-20 minutes.

5. Cover the dough with the sliced tomatoes. Sprinkle the cheese on top. Add the herbs.

Chopped ham, cheese and tomato

Corn, cheese and pineapple

Christmas tree cakes

For about 15 cakes, you will need:
1¼ cups self-rising flour
⅔ cup soft margarine
⅔ cup sugar
2 eggs
baking cups
muffin pan
assorted candy

For the butter icing:
⅓ cup butter or margarine, softened
1 cup powdered sugar, sifted
food dye
squeeze of lemon juice or a few drops of
vanilla extract

1. Follow steps 1 and 2 on page 10 to make some cake mix.

2. Put the baking cups in the muffin pan. Half-fill each one with cake mix.

3. Bake them for about 20 minutes. Leave them on a rack to cool.

4. To make the butter icing, stir the butter until it is creamy.

5. Add some of the powdered sugar. Stir it in. Mix in the rest, a little at a time.

6. Stir in a few drops of food dye and the lemon juice or vanilla.

7. Spread some icing on top of each cake. Put a piece of candy in the middle.

8. Put small pieces of candy around the middle one to make a pattern.

   Heat the oven to 375ºF

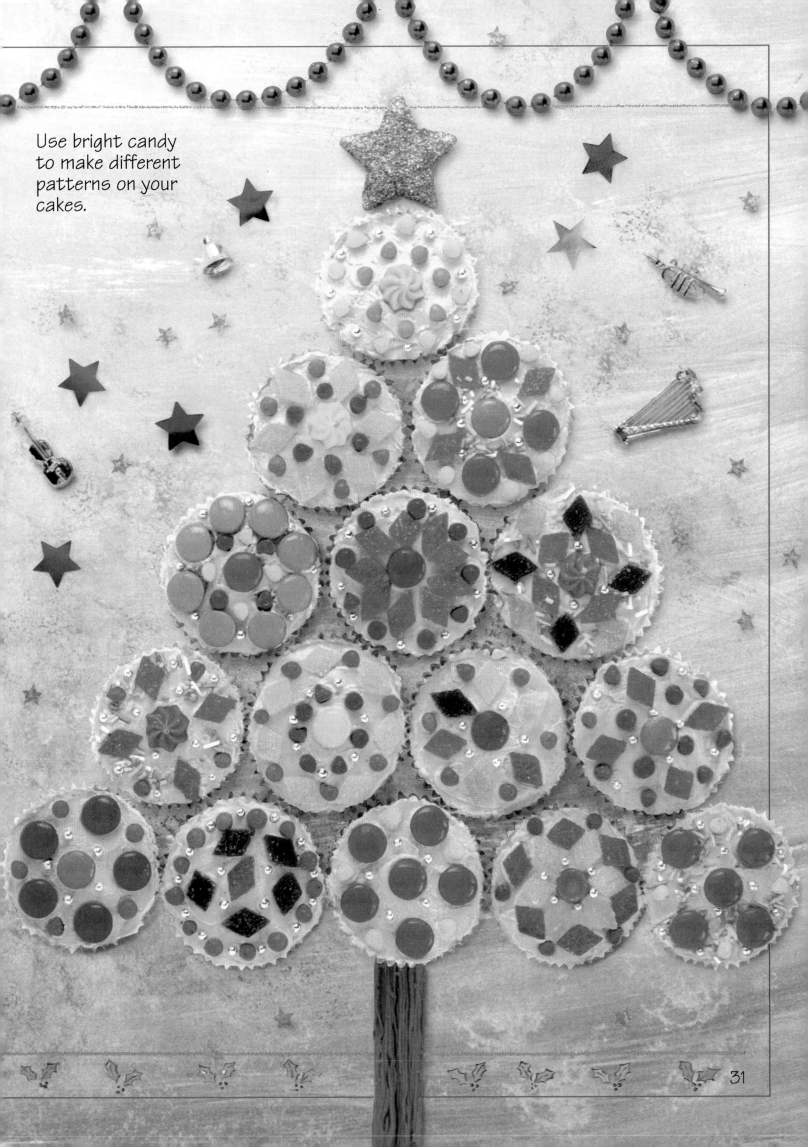

Use bright candy
to make different
patterns on your
cakes.

31

Sunshine toast

You will need:
1 slice of bread
margarine
1 medium or small egg
large cookie cutter
cookie sheet

1. Dip a paper towel into some margarine and rub it all over a cookie sheet.

2. Spread margarine on one side of the bread. Press the cutter hard in the middle of the bread.

3. Lift out the shape you have cut. Lay the pieces of bread on the tray, with the butter up.

4. Break the egg onto a saucer. Carefully slide the egg into the hole you have cut.

5. Bake for seven minutes on the top rack of an oven, or for a little longer if you don't like a runny yolk.

6. Lift the pieces of bread carefully off the tray. Eat it while it is warm.

What shall I be?

Contents

With thanks to Ben Bokaie, Raz Budeiri, Inigo Choong, Kezia Evans, Pippa Green, Jessica Hopf, James Jacob, Martha Kiff, Kattja Madrell, Emma Pearson, William Rowlands, Kyrie Simon-Penfold and Yasmin Wilson

A circus strongman

Print or paint shapes on material (see right).

1. Cut wavy ends in a piece of material. Dab big spots of orange paint all over with a sponge.

2. Dab black spots around the orange ones to look like leopard spots. Leave it to dry.

3. Tape a sponge to the top of each of your arms. Pull on a long-sleeved T-shirt over the top.

4. Pull on a pair of bright tights then put on a pair of dark shorts on top of them.

5. Put the spotted material over one shoulder. Fasten it around your waist with a belt.

6. Put some hair gel in your hair. Part your hair in the middle and smooth it down.

Make some weights

7. Dip a damp sponge in red face paint. Dab it lightly over your cheeks.

8. Use a brush and dark face paint to draw big eyebrows. Add a curly mustache.

1. Blow up two balloons. Paint two tubes from the middle of kitchen paper towels.

2. Use little pieces of tape to join the tubes together. Tape a balloon on at each end.

Print shapes on a bright undershirt with paint and a cookie cutter.

Face paint a hairy chest.

A scarecrow

1. Tape lots of clean dry straw or long grass inside an old hat.

2. Sponge brown face paint in patches on your face. Sponge red on your cheeks.

3. Brush on spiked eyebrows and a mustache with brown face paint.

4. Dab face paint on your nose and add big freckles. Brush red on your lips too.

5. Pull on a big checked shirt and some old pants or a skirt.

6. Put on some old boots or shoes. Put rubber bands around your ankles.

7. Put rubber bands around your wrists. Don't make them tight.

8. Push straw into your cuffs and pant legs, under the rubber bands.

Tie a bright scarf around your neck and pin a toy mouse to your hat.

Put a belt around your waist and push straw under it.

A snow queen

Make a crown

1. Glue and press foil inside the base of a big plastic bottle. Glue it outside if the bottle isn't clear.

2. Cut out four pieces of foil as big as this book. Cut each piece in two from end to end.

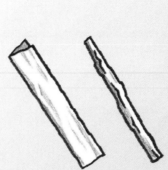

3. Fold each piece of foil in half like this. Squeeze each one into a long, thin shape.

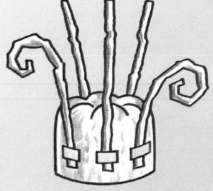

4. Tape five of the pieces evenly around the bottom of the crown. Curl the ends over.

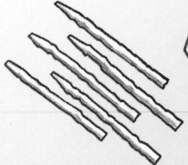

5. Cut the other pieces of foil in half. Pinch one end to make pointed icicles.

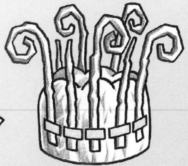

6. Tape five of the icicles around the bottle in between the long ones. There will be one icicle left.

7. Cut some foil as long as this book. Fold it over and over. Tape it around the bottom of the crown.

8. Wrap the spare icicle around one of your fingers for a ring. Twist the end into a spiral shape.

Snowflakes

1. Cut a small square of thin white or silver paper.

2. Fold the square diagonally to make a triangle. Fold it in half again.

3. Cut different shapes along each edge then open it out and flatten it.

A wand

Cover a thin stick in foil. Glue a snowflake to one end of it.

Press some self-adhesive stars onto your hair.

Use an old skirt or piece of material for a cloak. Glue or pin on some snowflakes and stars.

Attach the crown to your hair with bobby pins.

Fasten the cloak with a brooch.

39

A puppy

1. If your hair is short, tie a ribbon or a piece of elastic around your head.

2. Stuff a pair of short socks with plenty of cotton balls.

Long hair

1. If your hair is long, tie it into two high bunches.

3. Tuck the socks into the band. Use bobby pins to hold them in place.

4. Dab white face paint over your face. Close your eyes when you get near them.

2. Push each bunch into a short sock. Fasten them with bands.

5. Dab orange face paint on in patches. Brush black on the end of your nose.

6. Use a brush and brown face paint to add spots and big patches.

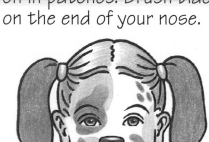

7. Brush a black line from your nose to your top lip. Brush along your lip too.

8. Add a red tongue on your bottom lip. Add dots on either side of your nose.

After you have painted your face, put socks on your hands and feet, for paws.

A lucky pirate

1. Sponge light brown face paint over your face.

2. Brush on big eyebrows and a curly mustache.

3. Dab stubble on your chin with a toothbrush.

4. Cut out an eyepatch shape from stiff black paper.

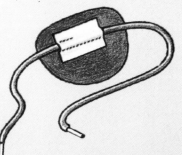

5. Tape a shoelace across the back of the eyepatch, near to the top.

6. Get someone to tie the eyepatch and knot a scarf around your head.

7. Slip a rubber band through a curtain ring. Hang it over your ear.

8. For a telescope, paint a cardboard tube. Put foodwrap over one end.

Use face paint to make a scar on your cheek.

Put some old necklaces and brooches in your treasure box too.

Make a treasure box

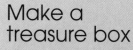

Find a box with a lid, like a chocolate or teabag box. Paint it.

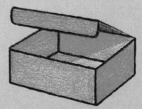

Cover things like bottle tops and cookies with foil to make treasure.

42

You could safety pin a toy parrot on your shoulder.

Face paint a curly beard instead of stubble.

Wear a leather belt across one shoulder.

43

A doctor

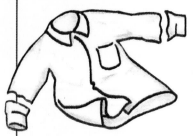

1. For a doctor's coat, use an old white shirt. Cut the sleeves to fit.

2. Push the lenses out of old sunglasses. Wear the frames.

3. For medicine, fill plastic bottles with water. Add a few drops of food dye.

4. Use a pillow for a bed. Fold a pillowcase in half for a top sheet.

Make a stethoscope

1. Cut a piece of foil twice as long as this book. Fold it in half.

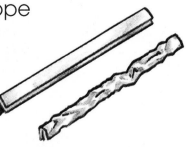

2. Fold the foil in half again then scrunch it up tightly.

3. Fold the foil in half. Pull the two ends apart and bend them in.

4. Cut a piece of foil as big as this book. Fold it and scrunch it up.

Use a lunch box for a doctor's case.

Make bandages from strips of material.

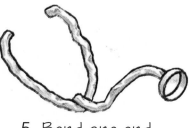

5. Bend one end around the long piece. Tape a jar lid on the other end.

Make a thermometer

Cut a strip of foil. Wrap it around the end of a straw and tape it on.

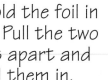

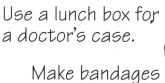

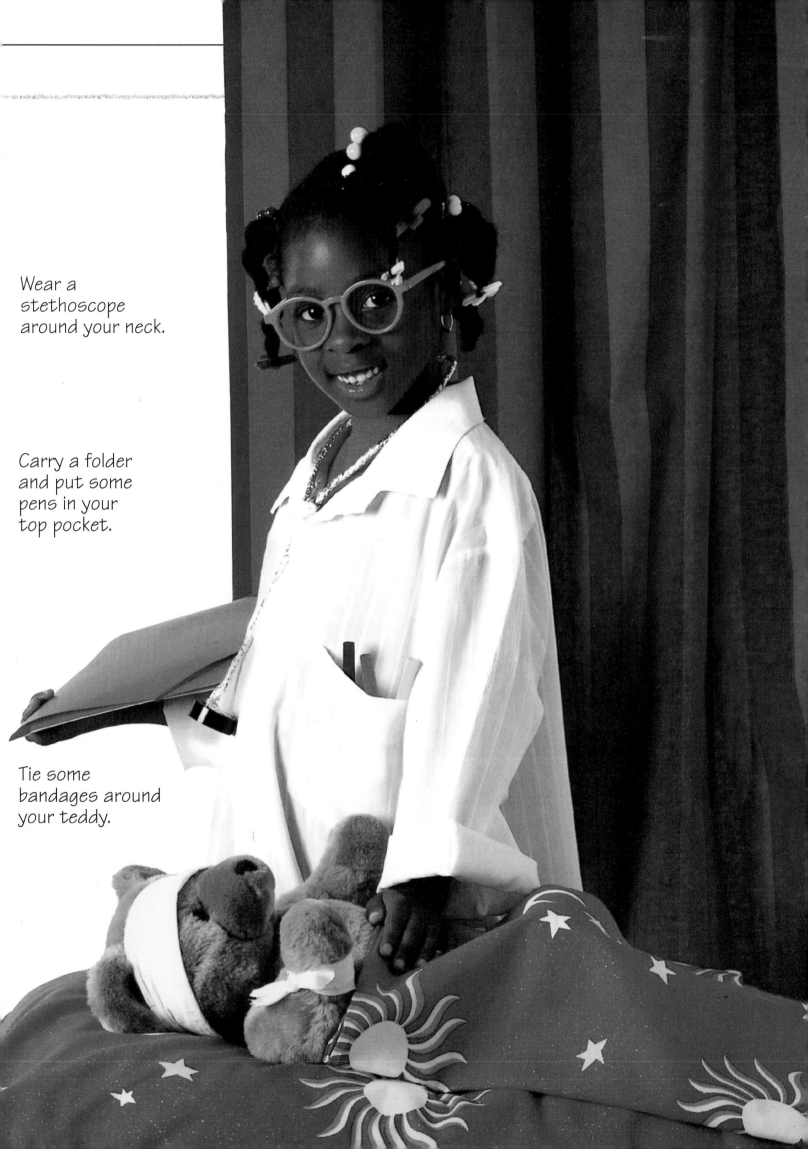

Wear a stethoscope around your neck.

Carry a folder and put some pens in your top pocket.

Tie some bandages around your teddy.

A spotted bug

1. Put two ice
cream cones on
newspaper. Paint
them then leave
them to dry.

2. Cut a strip of
thin cardboard to
fit over the top of
your head. Glue
the cones onto it.

3. Bend the
cardboard around
your head. Fasten
it at each side
with bobby pins.

4. Put a blob of
hair gel onto your
hand. Lift up a big
clump of your hair
in your other hand.

Remember you can't
eat the cones once
they are painted.

5. Squeeze your gelled hand around a clump of hair and pull it up. Do this to more clumps of hair.

Put face paint on your hands and arms.

6. Rub a damp sponge in face paint. Dab it over your face. Leave gaps for spots.

7. Use a brush and a different face paint to draw the outlines of spots in the gaps.

8. Fill in the spots with a brush. Close your eye when you fill in any spots that are near it.

Cut out spots and tape them onto a bright T-shirt.

A rich lady

Make some paper money

1. Cut four pieces of newspaper as big as this book. Fold them in half like this.

2. Fold the top edge down to the bottom. Then fold the top down to the bottom again.

3. Open out each piece of paper. Cut carefully along all the lines you have folded.

4. Write numbers on each piece of paper with a felt-tip pen. Keep them in a purse.

Carry lots of bright shiny things in a purse.

5. Pull on a bright T-shirt and a long floaty skirt. Put a belt around your waist.

6. Put on bright lipstick. Dab some pink powder or face paint on your cheeks.

7. Put on several necklaces, brooches and some big earrings. Wear a watch.

Carry a toy dog. Tie a belt around its neck for a lead.

Put on some sunglasses.

Wear a long scarf around your shoulders for a shawl.

8. Wrap a ribbon around a big hat. Use a safety pin to attach some big flowers on the side.

9. Scrunch up some paper and push it into the toes of a pair of high-heeled shoes.

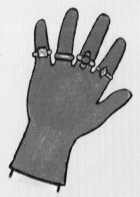

10. Put on the shoes and the hat. Put on some gloves and wear lots of rings on top of them.

Carry a purse.

A funny clown

1. Sponge white all over your face. Draw red circles on your cheeks and nose.

Wear a bright T-shirt. Cut buttons from felt or paper and tape or glue them on.

2. Brush a big smiling shape around your mouth and fill it in.

3. Brush two arch shapes over your eyes and fill them in carefully.

Wear pants that are too big for you. Use safety pins to attach ribbons, for suspenders.

4. Carefully draw black lines across your eyes. Add thin eyebrows.

Make a clown hat

1. Cut a roll of bright crêpe paper as wide as this book.

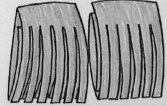

2. Cut the paper in two. Make cuts nearly to the top of each piece.

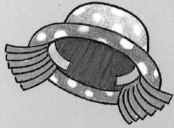

3. Tape the uncut edges inside a big hat. Tape them on at the sides.

4. Shake the hat to fluff out the hair. Tape on a fake flower at one side.

Big bow tie

1. Cut a piece of crêpe paper the same size as this book.

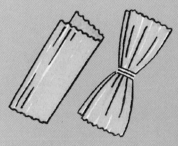

2. Fold it in half, long sides together. Put a rubber band around the middle.

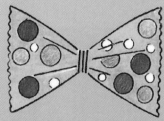

3. Stretch out the two ends. Press on self-adhesive or gummed shapes.

4. Put a safety pin through the rubber band and fasten it onto your clothes.

A chef on television

Make a chef's hat

1. Cut a strip of white cardboard as tall as your hand and which fits around your head.

2. Cut a piece of white crêpe paper so it is the same length as the cardboard.

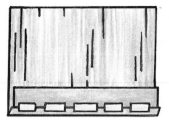

3. Lay the cardboard near the bottom of the paper. Fold the bottom edge over and tape it in place.

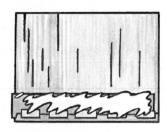

4. Put glue on the cardboard. Fold the cardboard over onto the crêpe paper and press it flat.

5. Hold the paper at each side. Pull your hands apart gently to stretch the paper like this.

6. Bend the cardboard around your head. Use small pieces of tape to join the ends.

7. Gather the top edge of the paper together and wrap a rubber band around it.

8. Press down the top of your hat so that it is flat on top. Puff it out around the sides.

Joke sausages

1. Carefully cut one leg from an old pair of pink or brown tights.

2. Squeeze four sheets of toilet paper to make a sausage shape.

3. Roll four pieces of paper around the sausage. Push it into the tights.

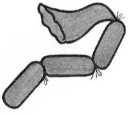

4. Tie thread at the end of the sausage. Make more sausages the same way.

Dressing up

Brush on a mustache with face paint. Add a little beard.

Put on an apron. Dip your fingers in flour and dab them over the apron.

Act as if you are doing a television show about cooking.

Dab some flour on your nose.

Collect some bowls, pans and spoons from your kitchen. Put them on a table in front of you.

53

Cinderella

Before

Pull some wispy pieces from cotton balls and put it in your hair, as cobwebs.

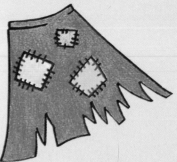

1. Cut the bottom of an old skirt into rags. Sew or use safety pins to add bright patches.

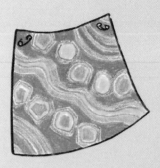

2. Use a safety pin to fasten a piece of bright material around your waist as an apron.

3. Fold a scarf like this. Wrap it around your shoulders and knot the ends in front of you.

4. Sponge some pink face paint on your cheeks. Add some grey for dirty patches.

Make a broom

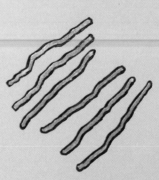

1. Collect lots of thin twigs. Snap them so that they are all about the same length.

2. Make them into a bunch around a stick. Wrap string around and around then tie it.

After

1. Pull on some pale tights and put on a pretty undershirt, leotard or swimsuit.

2. Tie some elastic around your waist. Tuck a piece of lace into it for a skirt.

3. Tie a strip of material or a piece of ribbon around your waist to hide the elastic.

4. For gloves, cut halfway down the legs of some old lacy tights. Cut the toes off too.

Paint your face

1. Dip a paintbrush in red face paint. Brush red flowers on your forehead and on your cheeks.

2. Brush a bow near each eyebrow and wavy lines between the flowers. Add green leaves too.

Tie bows on your shoulders and in your hair.

Glue fake flowers to your skirt.

Cinderella's sisters

Make a wig

1. Cut a piece from a roll of cotton as wide as this page. Then cut it into eight pieces.

2. Twist each piece to make ringlets. Clip them to your hair in front of your ears.

3. Cut another piece of cotton and clip it over your head to cover your hair.

4. Pull the cotton a little to make it lumpy. Glue on a big, bright gift-wrapping bow.

Paint your face

1. Sponge pale pink face paint all over your face. Make your cheeks a darker pink.

For a bright wig, dab paint on the cotton and let it dry before you put it on.

2. Brush on long eyelashes. Put on some very bright lipstick and add a beauty spot.

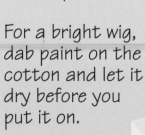

Make a fan

1. Cut a piece of gift wrap so that it is as wide as this book and twice as long.

2. Fold over one of the short edges. Turn the gift wrap over then fold the edge up again.

3. Keep folding the gift wrap over and over in this way until you get to the end of it.

4. Wrap some tape around it at the bottom. Snip shapes out at the top. Open it out.

Instead of a wig, make two braids from yarn. Use bobby pins to clip them to your hair.

Tie a scarf around your head to hide the ends of the braids.

Long nails

Cut ten pointed shapes from adhesive paper. Press them over your own nails.

Put on some necklaces and rings.

A long-armed giant

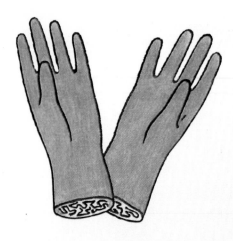

1. Scrunch up paper and push it into a pair of rubber gloves to make them stiff.

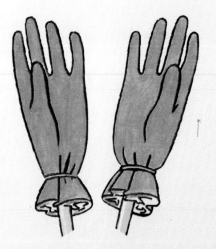

2. Push in the round ends of two wooden spoons. Fasten them with rubber bands.

3. Push a cushion up under your T-shirt to make a very fat belly.

4. Put a big sweater over your T-shirt. Fasten a belt around your waist.

5. Dip a damp sponge in red face paint and dab it on your nose and cheeks.

6. Wet a brush and dip it into dark face paint. Draw on bushy eyebrows.

7. Face paint wiggly shapes across your chin to make a curly beard.

8. Add dark freckles across your nose and paint white teeth on your bottom lip.

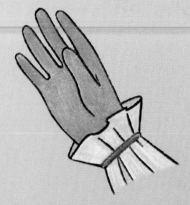

9. Pull your cuffs over the ends of the gloves. Fasten them with rubber bands.

Wear big boots and a vest.

Hold the handles of the spoons when you move your arms.

59

A very old person

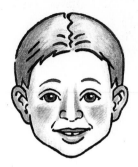

1. Brush your hair back. Use a sponge to stroke grey or white face paint over your hair.

2. Dip the sponge in pale pink or white face paint and dab it all over your face.

3. Dab dark pink over your cheeks. Then dab some brown down each side of your nose.

4. Use a brush and brown face paint to add some thin lines across your forehead.

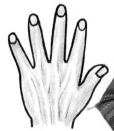

5. Brush two thin brown lines at the top of your nose, between your eyebrows.

6. Add a line from each side of your nose to your mouth. Smudge the lines with your finger.

7. Dip a toothbrush in grey and dab it on your face for stubble, or put on bright lipstick.

8. Brush thin blue or white lines on the back of your hands.

Collect some things like these to wear or carry.

For glasses, get someone to help you to take the lenses out of an old pair of sunglasses.

Wrap a scarf around your neck and wear a hat.

Painting your face

You can use face painting crayons, but the face paints which look like a box of paints are the best to use.

1. Make sure that your face is clean and dry. Put on the dressing-up clothes you are going to wear.

2. Wrap a towel around your neck to protect your clothes. Tie your hair back or put on a hairband.

3. To cover your face in face paint, dip a sponge in water then squeeze it until no more water comes out.

4. Rub the sponge around and around in the face paint. Dab it all over your face, right up to your hair.

Scarecrow
- page 36

5. Close each eye and dab over your eyelids very carefully. Press the sponge over your lips too.

Cinderella
- page 54

6. Wash your sponge and dip it into a different shade of face paint. Dab it lightly all over your cheeks.

7. Gently rub a thin wet paintbrush around in a face paint. Draw on eyebrows with the tip of the brush.

8. Use a thin paintbrush to add very fine lines on your forehead, around your eyes and on your cheeks.

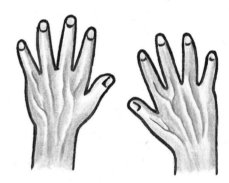

9. Use a paintbrush to add glitter face paint. Press little stars into it. They will stick as the paint dries.

10. Use face paint on your lips too. Brush around the shape of your lips then fill them in.

11. You can also put face paint on your hands and arms. Use a sponge to dab it on. Add lines with a brush.

Giant
- page 58

Clown
- page 50

Things you need

You will need face paints for most of the projects.

Strongman
yellow material
a belt
a long-sleeved T-shirt
two small sponges
a pair of shorts
hair gel
two balloons
two cardboard tubes
tape

Scarecrow
clean, dry straw or long
   grass
an old hat
old pants or a skirt
checked shirt
old boots or shoes
rubber bands

Snow queen
3 liter plastic bottle
kitchen foil
white or silver paper
a thin stick

Puppy
a pair of short socks
cotton balls and a
   ribbon or some
   elastic (if your hair
   is short)
bobby pins
a ribbon
mittens

Pirate
stiff black paper
a shoelace
a bright scarf

Pirate: continued
a curtain ring
rubber band
a small box
things for treasure
a cardboard tube
plastic foodwrap

Doctor
an old white shirt
old sunglasses
plastic bottles
food dye
pillow and two pillowcases
kitchen foil
a jar lid
a straw

Spotted bug
two ice cream cones
a strip of cardboard
paint
bobby pins
hair gel

Rich lady
a bright T-shirt
a long skirt
jewelry
a purse
lipstick
face powder
newspaper

Funny clown
crêpe paper
big bright hat
self-adhesive or gummed
   shapes
a safety pin

A television chef
white cardboard
white crêpe paper
toilet paper
old brown or pink tights
thread
flour
striped apron

Cinderella
an old skirt
scraps of material
a big scarf
a brooch
thin twigs and a stick
pale tights
a undershirt, leotard or
   swimsuit
elastic and ribbon
a lace

Cinderella's sisters
roll of cotton
bobby pins
bright gift-wrapping bow
gift wrap
adhesive paper
old lacy tights

Long-armed giant
a pair of rubber gloves
two wooden spoons
a cushion
a belt
a big sweater
rubber bands

Very old person
old sunglasses
hat and scarf

What shall I grow?

Contents

With thanks to John Russell

Green-haired creatures

1. Wet an old sock and put it into a mug. Turn the top over the rim.

2. Use a spoon to spread lots of grass seeds all over the bottom.

3. Use an old spoon to fill the mug with potting soil.

4. Wrap a rubber band tightly around the sock. Chop off the top.

5. Pour water onto the top of the sock. Lift it up and let it drip.

6. Turn it upside down. Put it on a saucer and pour water around.

7. For a nose, carefully push a pin through one of the holes in a button.

To make a porcupine, squash the sock into a pointy shape.

8. For eyes, push in some more pins with buttons near the nose.

9. Put your creature into a warm, light room. Make sure you keep the top wet.

You can cut the 'hair' short and let it grow again.

A giant sunflower

1. You need to buy a packet of sunflower seeds. Put stones into the bottom of a small pot.

2. Fill the pot with potting soil. Press in two seeds. Leave a gap between them.

3. Water your pot. Put it outside in a light place. Water it often to stop it from drying out.

4. Two seedlings should grow. Pull out the smaller one so that the other one grows well.

5. When the plant is about as high as your hand, get help to plant it in a bigger pot.

6. Water your plant and leave in a light sunny spot, which is out of the wind.

Look on the seed packet to see how tall your flower might grow.

7. When your plant is as high as your knee, push a cane into the soil. Tie the stem on.

8. As the plant grows taller, carefully tie its stem to the cane higher up.

 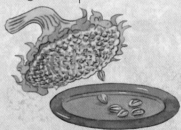

9. When the petals fall from the flower, leave the seeds on the plant to grow and ripen.

10. Shake out a few seeds from the head to plant next year. Leave the rest for the birds to eat.

Sunflowers have huge flowers and can grow very tall.

Plant your seeds in the spring.

Your plants will grow flowers in summer.

A tiny yard

Use small plants such as pansies, primula, ivy, trailing lobelia and alyssum.

1. Get someone to help you to make holes in the bottom of an old plastic dishpan.

2. Cover the bottom of the pan with small pebbles or pieces of broken pots.

3. Use a small spade to fill the pan almost to the top with potting soil.

4. For a pond, make a hole in the soil. Put a shallow plastic carton into it.

5. Put small pebbles into the bottom of the carton. Fill it with water.

6. Cut a lawn from a piece of sod. Put it beside the pond and water it well.

7. Dig small holes and plant a mixture of small plants around your lawn and pond.

8. Put some plastic dolls' house furniture onto the lawn. Add a tiny cat or dog too.

Plant this at any time.

Sprout shapes

1. Tear off ten paper towels. Lay them on a large flat plate or a small plastic tray.

2. Use a spoon to put water on the paper towels. Add water until they are soaking.

3. Lay some cookie cutters on the towels with their sharp edges pointing down.

4. Use a teaspoon to sprinkle lots of alfalfa seeds into each shape. Do this carefully.

You can eat the alfalfa you have grown. Try it in an egg sandwich or a salad.

You can grow these at any time. They will grow in four to five days.

5. Spread the seeds all over each shape with your fingers. Hold the cutter as you do it.

6. Lift the cutters off the towel leaving the seed shapes. Put them in a light place.

7. Use a spoon to water around the seeds every day. Don't put water on the seeds.

8. When the alfalfa is as long as your little finger, cut it off so you can eat it.

Tiny islands in the sea

1. Cut the top off some vegetables which have sprouted a little. Cut them as thick as this.

Use vegetables such as carrots, parsnips, turnips and beets.

2. Put a little cold water into a shallow dish. Spread the vegetable tops over the bottom.

3. Carefully pour in a little more water around the vegetable tops but don't cover them.

4. Put the dish on a windowsill. Add a little water each day. The shoots will grow in a few days.

Your shoots should grow to look like tall trees on islands.

You can grow these at any time.

A spiky plant

1. Cut the top off a pineapple so that the yellow part of it is as thick as this.

2. Lay it on its side on a plate. Leave it on a windowsill for two days so that it dries out a little.

3. Fill a pot with potting soil. Put the pineapple top on top. Press more soil around.

4. Water it and leave it in a warm place. New leaves will grow in the middle.

Water your pineapple plant often.

Grow when you can buy a ripe pineapple.

Crocuses in a silver pot

1. Turn a pot upside down and lay some kitchen foil over it. Make a hole in the top of the foil.

2. Turn the pot over. Press the edges of the foil inside the top of the pot.

3. Use a spoon to put potting soil into the pot. Fill it about halfway up the pot.

4. Put some crocus corms (which look like bulbs) into the pot with their pointed ends up.

5. Fill the pot almost to the top with more soil. Water it so that it is damp.

6. Put the pot into a cool, dark place. Look at it once a week. Water it if it feels dry.

Cut shapes from paper and glue them on the foil.

7. When the shoots are as long as your thumb put the pot into a light, cool place. Keep it damp.

8. When the shoots grow taller, put the pot in a light place. The flowers will come out.

Plant in the fall to bloom in the spring. They take 10 to 12 weeks to grow.

When the flowers die, cut the heads off. Plant the corms in flower beds and they may flower again next year.

Stand your pot on a saucer to keep it from marking surfaces.

Try planting miniature daffodil bulbs in the same way.

Potatoes in a bucket

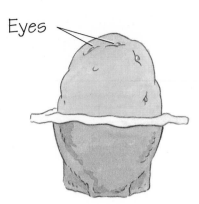

Eyes

1. Put a potato into an egg carton, with its eyes at the top. Leave it for several weeks until it grows shoots.

2. When the shoots are as long as this, rub off most of the shoots but leave two which look strong.

3. Make holes in the bottom of an old bucket. Cover the bottom with stones then add some potting soil.

4. Push the potato into the soil with the shoots pointing up. Cover it with soil. Leave it outside.

5. In about four weeks, you'll see some shoots. Cover them with soil and water your bucket.

6. Add more soil and water it every time the shoots appear. Do this until the bucket is full.

7. After a while, flowers will grow. Water your plant often. If a potato appears, cover it with some soil.

8. After four months the plant will die. Tip the bucket over. See how many potatoes have grown.

Don't forget to water your plant if the soil feels dry.

Keep your potatoes in a cool, dark place until you are ready to cook and eat them.

Pots of pansies

1. Rinse the bottom part of an egg carton under a faucet. Let it drip.

2. Put some potting soil in the sections. Don't fill them to the top.

3. Put two pansy seeds into each section. Leave a gap between them.

4. Sprinkle some more soil on top of the seeds and press it down.

5. Cover the carton with a newspaper and leave it outside in a cool place.

6. Keep the seeds moist. After about two weeks, shoots will begin to show.

7. Take off the newspaper so that the shoots can get plenty of light.

For pansies which will flower in winter, plant in the late summer.

8. When they have grown two leaves, pull out the smaller shoot.

9. As your pansies grow, roots will grow through the sides of the carton.

10. Soak the carton and gently pull the sections apart.

11. Half-fill a pot with soil. Put one section into it. Add more soil.

12. Put your pots outside on warm days, but bring them in at night.

You can plant your pansies straight into a flower bed if you like.

Paint your pots with acrylic paint if you like.

Roots and shoots

1. Soak a big jar and peel off its labels. Soak three lima beans in a saucer.

2. Rinse the inside of the jar with cold water. Empty it out but don't dry it.

3. Fold a paper napkin in half. Curl it into a circle and slip it inside the jar.

4. Press the napkin against the side of the jar with the handle of a spoon.

5. Peel back part of the napkin. Push a lima bean in against the jar.

You can grow these at any time. They take two to three weeks.

6. Add the other beans around the jar. Wet the napkin with lots of water.

7. Put the jar in a bright, warm place. Add water often to keep the napkin wet.

Leafy stems

1. You need a pot or a mug and some florist's foam (the kind used to arrange flowers in a vase).

2. Soak the foam in a bowl of water. Leave it in the water until bubbles stop coming to the surface.

3. Push the foam into your pot. Use scissors to trim it so that it is a little bit below the top of the pot.

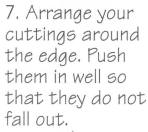

4. Ask if you can cut pieces from plants which have woody stems. Make them just longer than your hand.

5. The pieces you have cut are called cuttings. Snip a straight end just below a leaf of each cutting.

6. Pull off the bottom leaves. Push the end of the stem into the foam near to the edge.

7. Arrange your cuttings around the edge. Push them in well so that they do not fall out.

8. Put your pot on a windowsill but out of very bright sunshine. Water the foam often to keep it damp.

9. When new leaves grow, take the foam out of the pot and look and see if roots have grown.

10. Take a blunt knife and carefully cut the foam away from each cutting. Try not to damage their roots.

11. Plant each cutting in a pot full of potting soil. Water it and put it outside in a warm, light place.

Do this in the fall. They will grow in 6-8 weeks.

When you plant your cuttings, make sure that you don't forget to water them.

Cuttings in foam.

Rosemary

Box

Sage

Lavender

Ivy

You can plant more than one ivy cutting in a pot.

Bean sprouts to eat

1. Put two large spoons of mung beans into a strainer. Rinse them.

2. Soak the beans overnight in cold water. They will swell a little.

3. Lay some cotton on a plastic tray. Put water on it to make it damp.

Eat your mung beans in a crunchy salad.

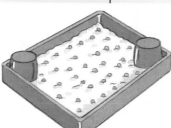

4. Put two egg cups upside down onto the tray. Spread the beans all over.

5. Slide the tray into a plastic bag then put it in a black trash bag. Put it in a very warm, dark place.

6. Check each day that the cotton has not dried out. Water it to keep it damp.

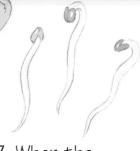

7. When the shoots are this long, pull them off the cotton. Rinse them well.

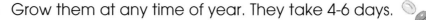

Tasty tomatoes

1. You will need to buy two or three small tomato plants. Get them from a garden center.

2. For each plant, put stones into a big plant pot. Cover them with potting soil.

3. Gently tip each plant out of its pot. Put one in each big pot. Try not to squash the leaves.

4. Add more soil to fill the pot. Gently press the soil around each plant with your fingers.

5. Water your plants well and leave them outside in a sunny place. Bring them in if it is frosty.

6. Water your plants every day, especially if it is hot and sunny. Flowers will grow.

7. As your plants grow taller, carefully push a cane into the pot and tie the stem to it.

8. After the flowers have died, little tomatoes will grow. Pick them when they turn red.

Plant them in spring and you'll get tomatoes in summer.

A leaf into a plant

1. Fill a small bottle with water. Don't fill it quite to the top so that you leave a small space.

2. Cut a paper square and fasten it over the top of the bottle with a rubber band.

3. Use scissors to cut off a leaf with its stalk from an African violet.

4. The leaf should be from near the outside and should look healthy.

Leave your plant in a light place, but not on a very sunny windowsill.

Grow at any time.

5. Hold the bottle. Make a hole in the middle of the paper with a very sharp pencil.

6. Push the stalk through the hole. Its end should go in the water. Add more water if you need to.

7. When tiny roots grow and new leaves appear it is ready to plant in a pot.

8. Make a hole in some soil. Put the plant in it and gently press around it. Water your plant.

Put your pot on a saucer. When you water it, put the water in the saucer, not on the plant.

Herbs on your windowsill

1. Buy some fresh herbs which are growing in a pot from a supermarket.

2. Wash out some empty half liter (one pint) milk cartons. You will need one for each herb.

3. Dry the cartons. Snip halfway down one side. Then cut the top off all the way around.

4. Turn each carton over. Make a hole in the bottom with the point of a sharp pencil.

5. Put some stones into the bottom of each carton. Spoon in a little potting soil.

6. Take each herb out of its pot by tipping it over and tapping the bottom of the pot.

Chives

Dill

7. Fill the gap between the carton and the roots with soil. Press the top of the soil.

8. Cut a strip of paper long enough to go around and slightly wider than each carton.

9. Wrap one of the pieces of paper around each carton. Tape it at the back.

10. Put your herbs onto a tray and leave them on a windowsill. Keep the soil moist.

Parsley

Basil

Thyme

A sweet-smelling flower

Grow a hyacinth in soil

1. Use an old spoon to put potting soil into a pot. Don't fill it to the top.

2. Gently press the bulb in the middle, with the bud on top. Add more soil.

3. Stand the pot on a saucer. Carefully water around the bulb.

4. Put it in a cool, dark place for eight to ten weeks. Keep the soil damp.

5. When it has grown as high as your index finger, put it in a light, cool place.

6. When it grows a little taller, put it in a warm place. A flower will grow.

Grow a hyacinth in water

1. Cut two foil circles and lay them over a tumbler. Press the bulb on top.

2. Carefully press the foil down all around the sides of the tumbler.

3. Lift off the bulb. Make a 2.5cm (1in) slit in the middle of the foil.

Rubber band

4. Snip the slit to make an X. Fill the tumbler with water, up to the foil.

5. Sit the bulb on top of the X. Leave it in a cool, dark place.

6. When the roots have grown long, move your bulb into a cool, light room.

Plant several bulbs together in a bowl, but don't let them touch.

This is a special glass you can buy for growing a hyacinth.

An ivy tower

1. Put stones into a very large pot which has a hole in it. Fill the pot with potting soil.

2. Use a rubber band to fasten four short garden canes together near to one end, like this.

3. Spread out the canes. Push them well into the pot, with their ends nearly touching the sides.

4. Dig a small hole at the bottom of one of the canes. Put an ivy plant into the hole.

5. Add a little soil around the plant and press it down firmly with your knuckles.

6. Dig a hole at the bottom of the other three canes. Plant an ivy in each hole.

7. Hold the longest stem of each plant and twist it carefully around its cane. Water your plants.

8. As the ivy grows, twist each stem around its cane every two or three days.

    You can grow these at any time. They take 3-4 weeks.

Paint your pot with acrylic paint and put lots of Christmas decorations on your ivy tower.

A moss garden

1. Put a thin layer of potting soil into the bottom of a shallow tray, with no holes in the bottom of it.

2. Hunt for some moss on lawns, walls and between paving slabs. Look on stones and pieces of bark too.

3. Dig up small pieces of moss and put them on your tray. Add any mossy stones and pieces of bark.

4. Collect some rainwater if you can, but tap water will do, and spray the moss well every day.

Watch your mosses grow.

Add some shells too.

Grow at any time.

What shall I draw?

Contents

Draw a pig

1 2 3 4

5 6 7 8

Lying down pig

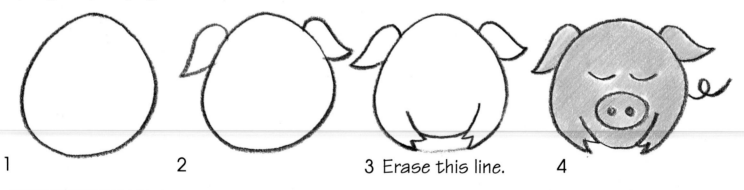

1 2 3 Erase this line. 4

Sideways pig

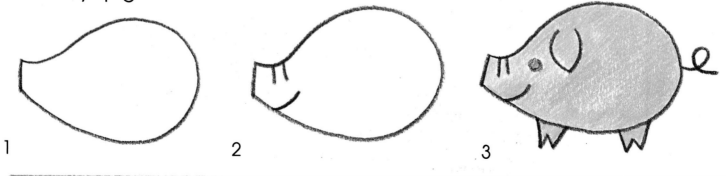

1 2 3

A piggy scene

You could draw any kind of flowers. These are tulips.

For lettuce leaves, draw wiggly green shapes.

Green spikes for grass

Wavy brown lines for mud

Now how about... a pig family at dinner time?

Draw a sea monster

What shall I draw today?

1

2

3

4

A sea monster battle

Soft blue crayoning for the sky

Drops of water

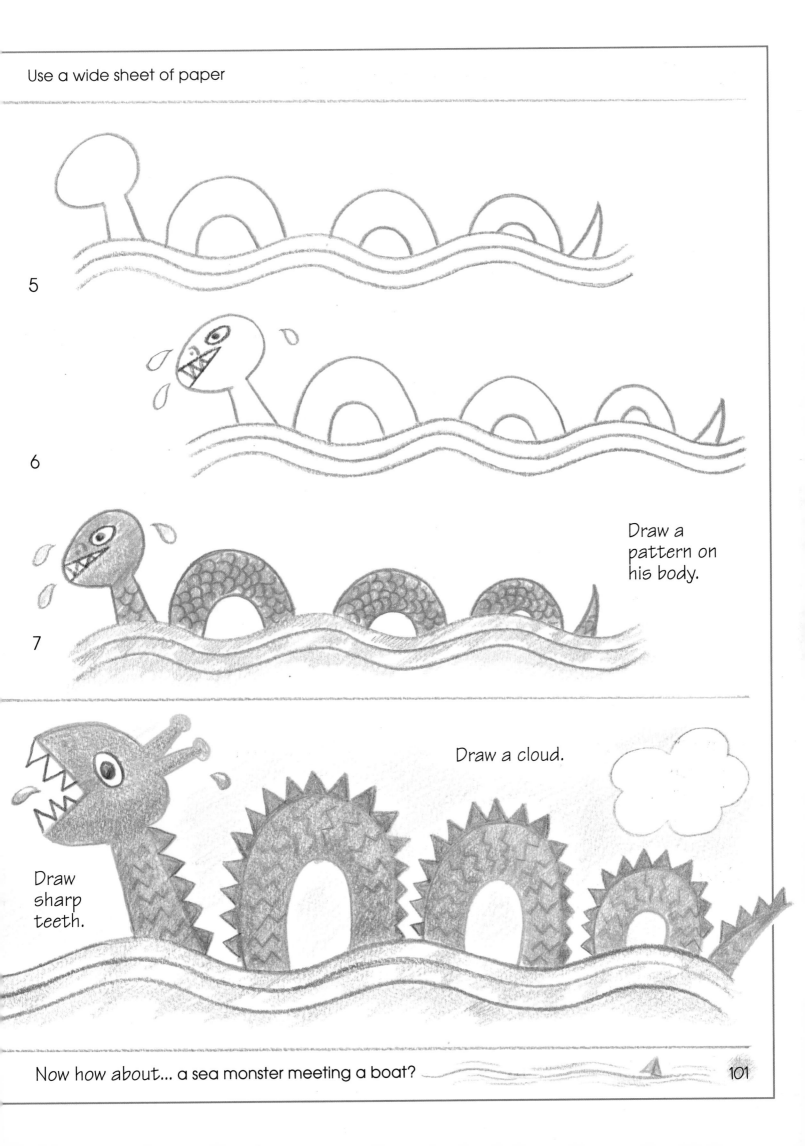

5

6

Draw a
pattern on
his body.

7

Draw a cloud.

Draw
sharp
teeth.

Draw a snail

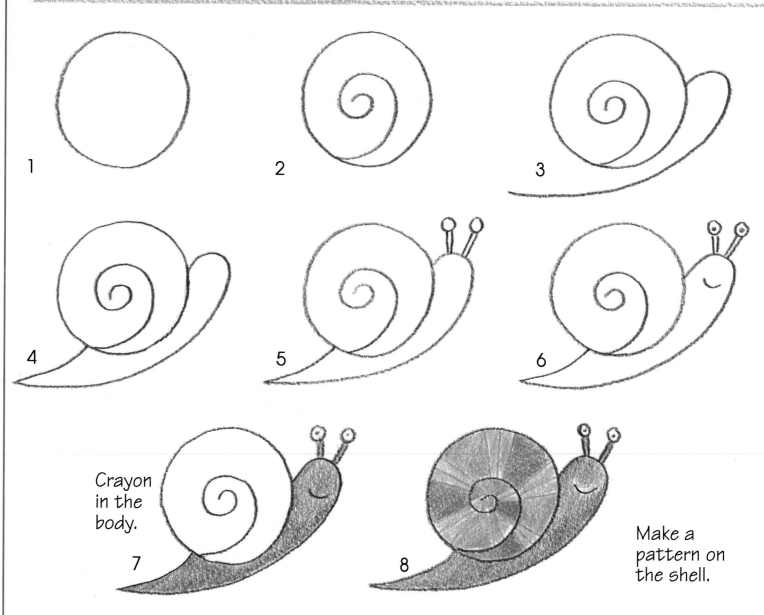

1

2

3

4

5

6

Crayon
in the
body.

7

8

Make a
pattern on
the shell.

Draw the children

Draw some little
baby snails.

Make the shells different.

Make a picture story

1

2

3

Draw snails on a flower.

Add some grass and leaves.

Open mouth

Jagged bite in the leaf

4

5

6

Now how about... A snail race?

Draw a space rocket

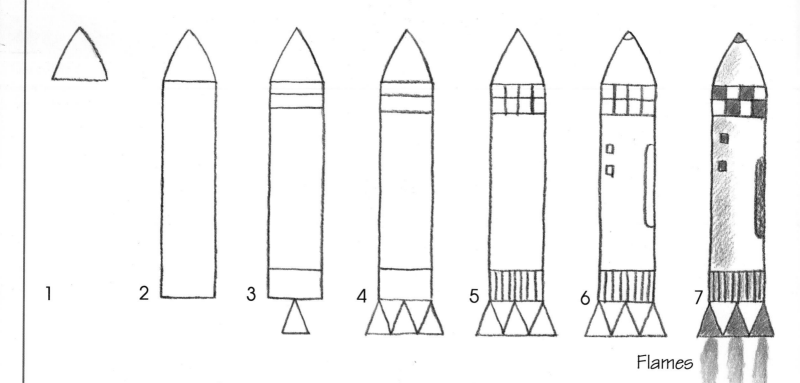

1   2   3   4   5   6   7

Flames

A rocket launch

1 Draw a tall ladder for the launch tower.

2

3

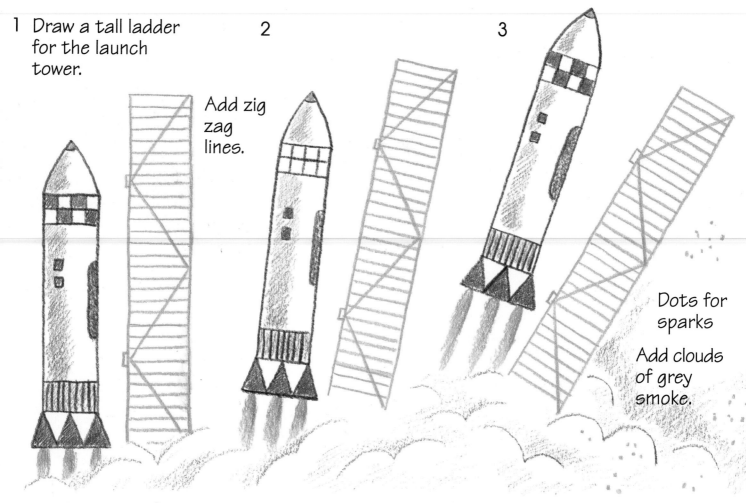

Add zig zag lines.

Dots for sparks

Add clouds of grey smoke.

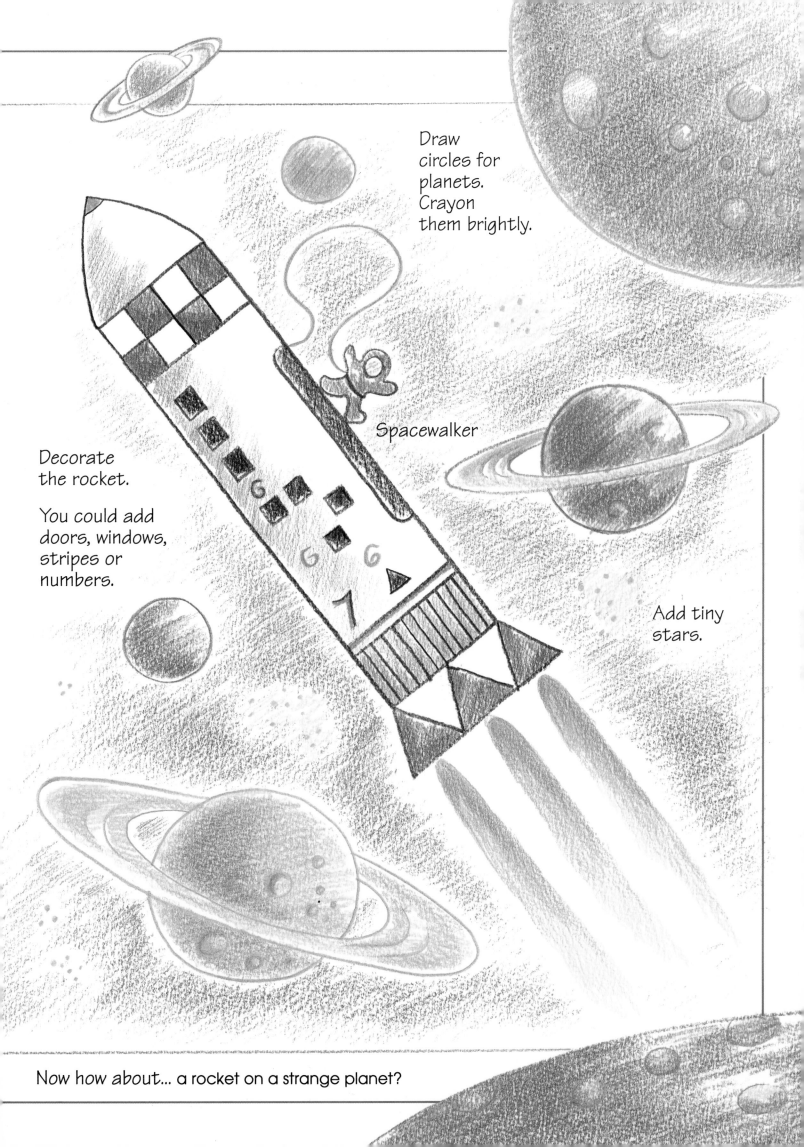

Draw circles for planets. Crayon them brightly.

Decorate the rocket.

You could add doors, windows, stripes or numbers.

Spacewalker

Add tiny stars.

Now how about... a rocket on a strange planet?

Draw an owl

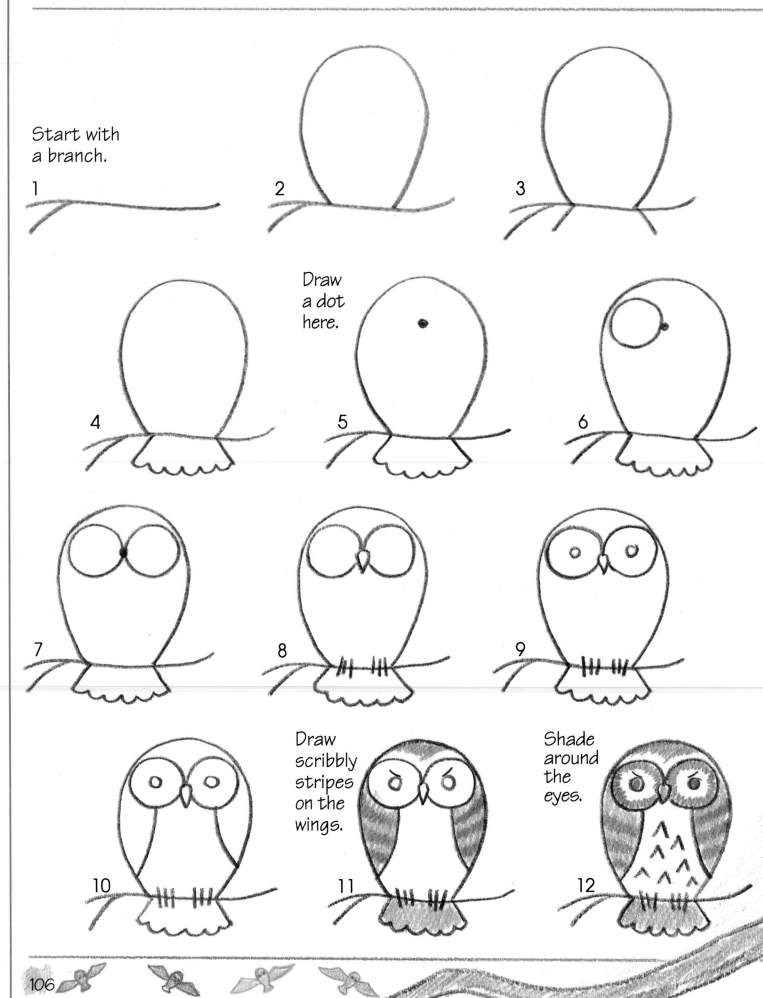

Start with a branch.

1

2

3

Draw a dot here.

4

5

6

7

8

9

Draw scribbly stripes on the wings.

Shade around the eyes.

10

11

12

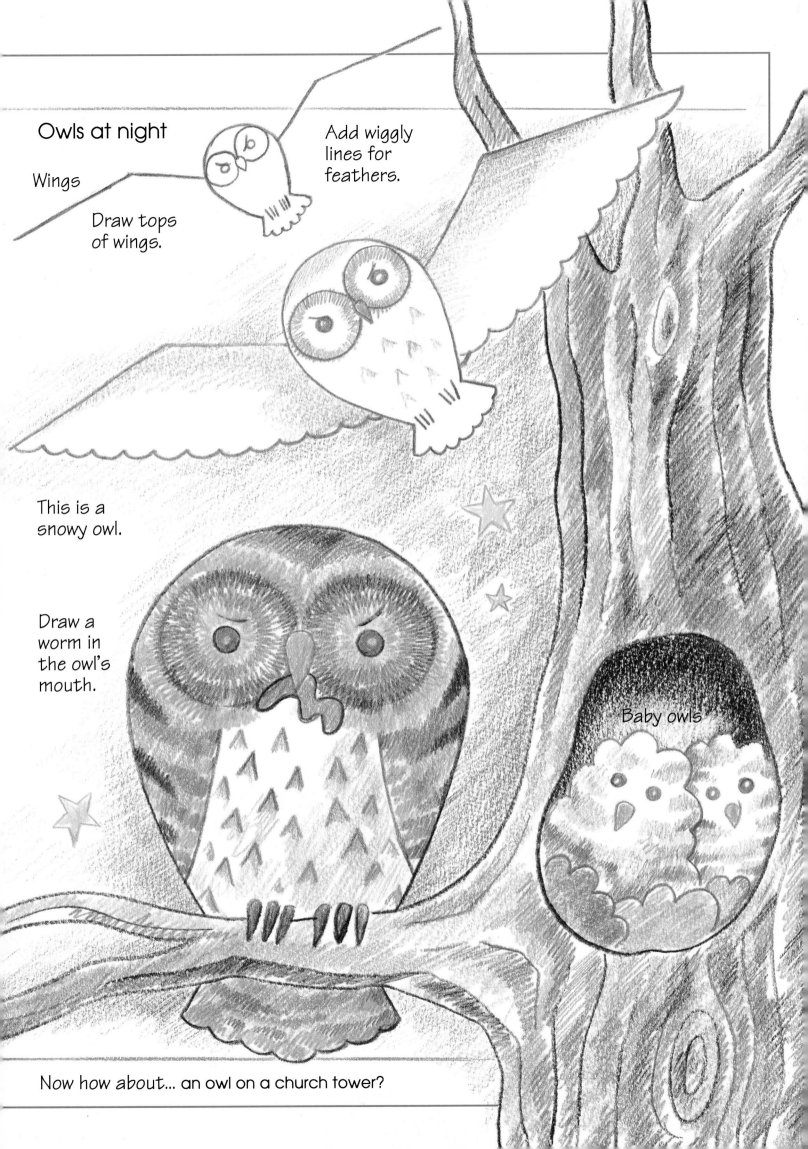

Owls at night

Wings

Draw tops of wings.

Add wiggly lines for feathers.

This is a snowy owl.

Draw a worm in the owl's mouth.

Baby owls

Now how about... an owl on a church tower?

Draw a submarine

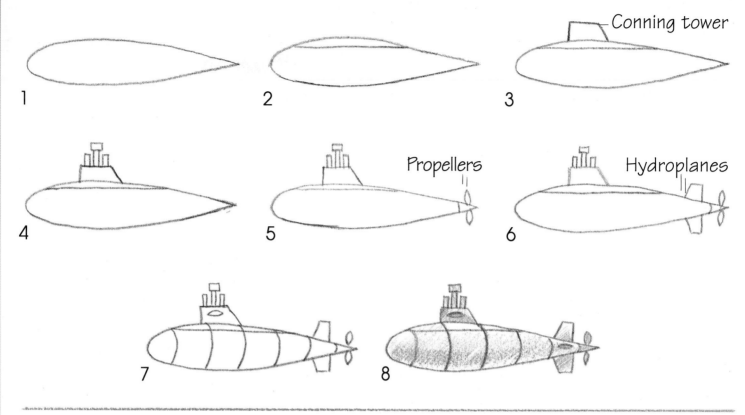

Conning tower

1

2

3

Propellers

Hydroplanes

4

5

6

7

8

Under the sea

Draw a battle with a giant octopus. Add sea creatures, shells and seaweed.

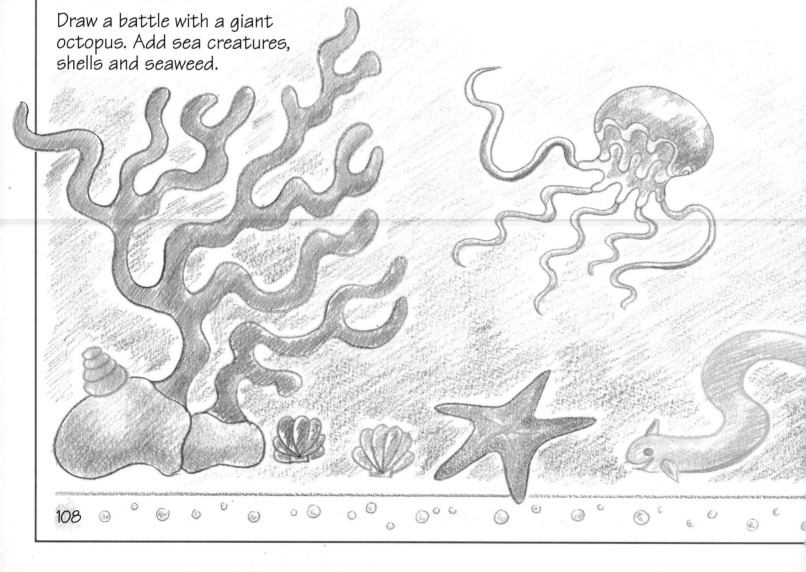

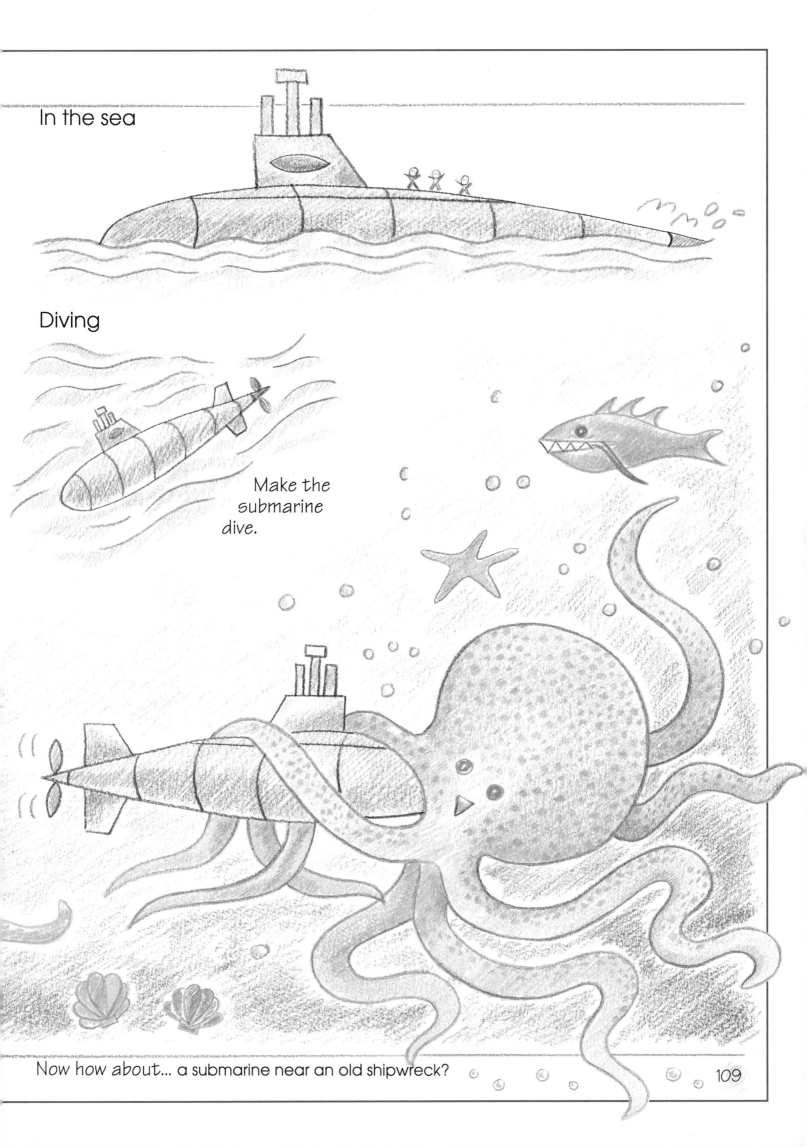

In the sea

Diving

Make the
submarine
dive.

Now how about... a submarine near an old shipwreck?

Draw a tiger

1

2

3

4

5

6

7

8

9

10 Erase the lines you don't need.

11 Crayon the body, but leave some white patches.

12 Add scribbly stripes.

Sleeping tiger

Leaping tiger

Draw a tree
for the tiger
to lie on.

Now how about... some tigers prowling in the grass?

111

Draw a wizard

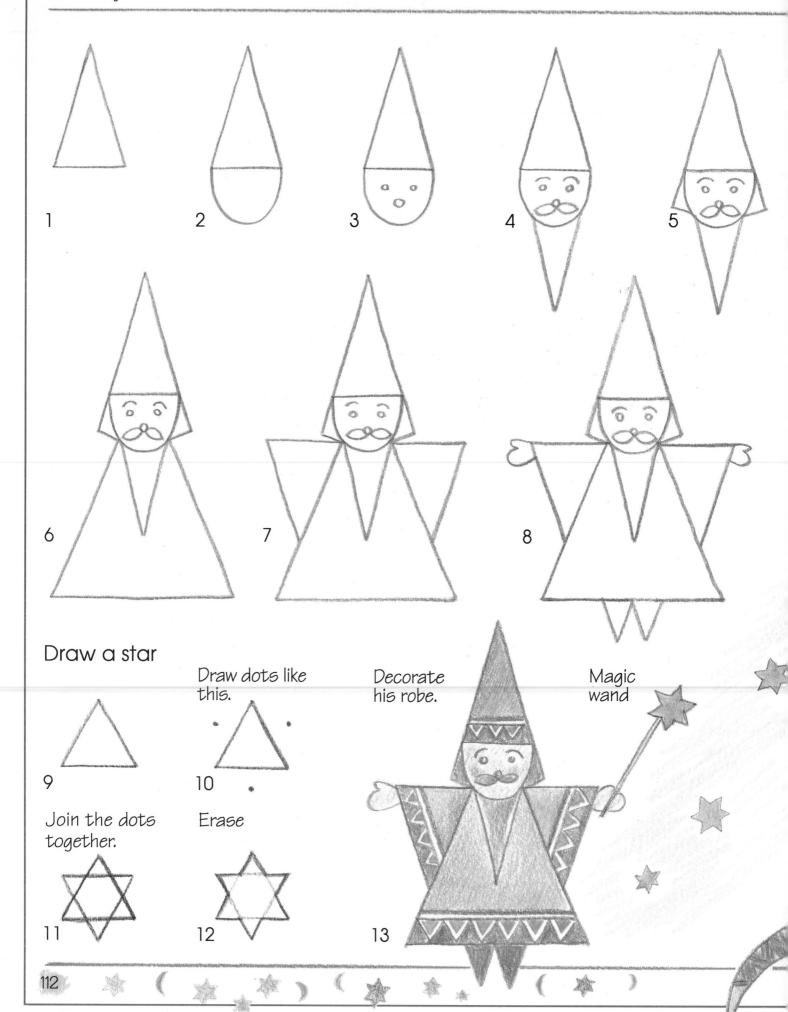

1

2

3

4

5

6

7

8

Draw a star

Draw dots like
this.

Decorate
his robe.

Magic
wand

9

10

Join the dots
together.

Erase

11

12

13

Draw some stars to show he is casting a spell.

Spell book

Snake

Cauldron

Draw a helicopter

1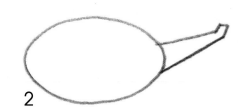

2

3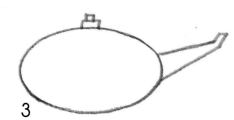

4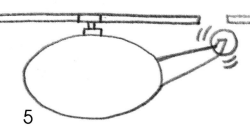

5

6

Lines around the tail propeller make it seem to move.

7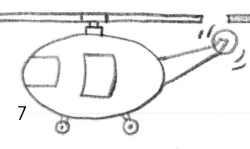

8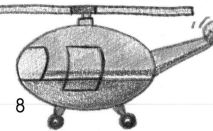

Crayon your helicopter.

More flying 'copters

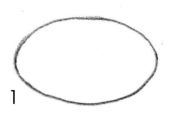

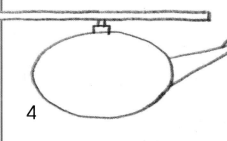

These helicopters are rescuing people.

This one has skids underneath, so it can land on the water.

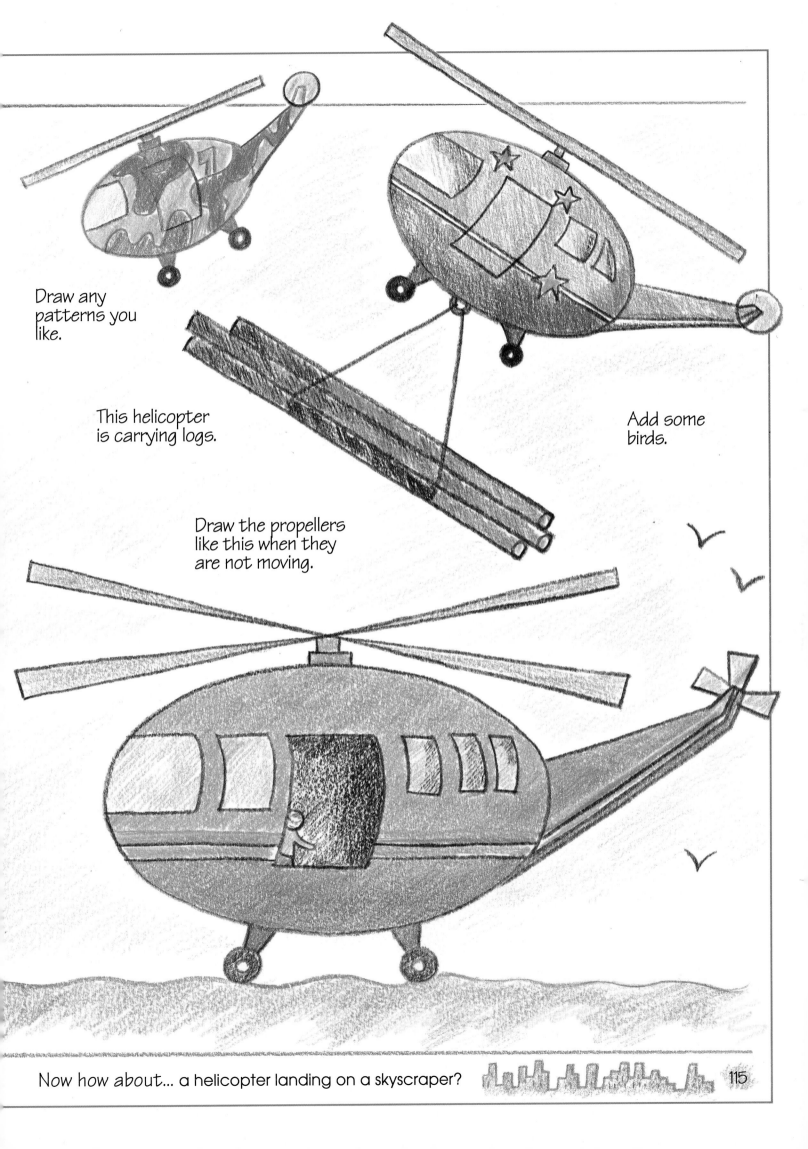

Draw any patterns you like.

This helicopter is carrying logs.

Draw the propellers like this when they are not moving.

Add some birds.

Now how about... a helicopter landing on a skyscraper?

Draw a cat

Snoozing cat

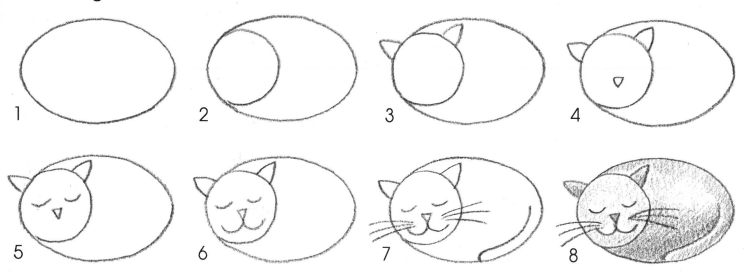

1 2 3 4

5 6 7 8

Standing cat

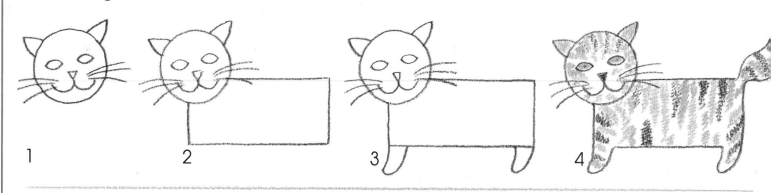

1 2 3 4

Crouching cat

1

Draw the body
in pencil first.

2

Erase one end.
Draw in the head.

Lapping cat

Add a
tongue and
a saucer of
milk.

3

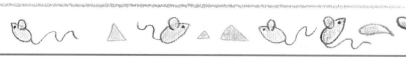

Sitting cat

1

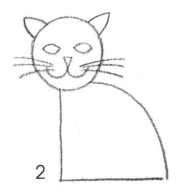

2

3

4

Cat family

Draw a large
sitting cat
for the
mother.

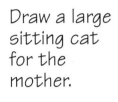

Don't
forget
their
tails.

Comfy cat

Draw the snoozing cat
on a cushion.

Now draw the kittens.
Add two paws beneath
each head.

Draw a box for the kittens.

Now how about... a cat on a roof...a cat chasing a mouse?

Draw circles

Try drawing circles. If it's too hard, you could draw around a cup.

Dinner

Fish

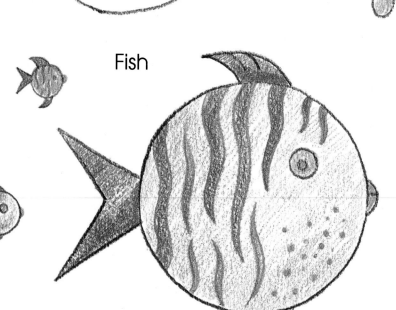

Snowman

Robin

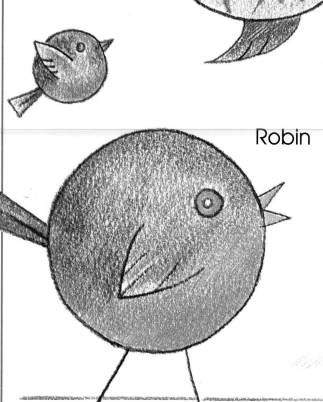

Apple

Clock

Balloon

Mouse

Lion

Now how about... a spider?... what else can you think of?

119

Draw a clown

1

2

3

4

5

6 Erase this line.

7

8

Clowning around

You
could
draw the
arms in
different
positions.

Decorate
the clown
however
you like.

Add
some
balls for
a juggling
clown.

Draw a ballerina

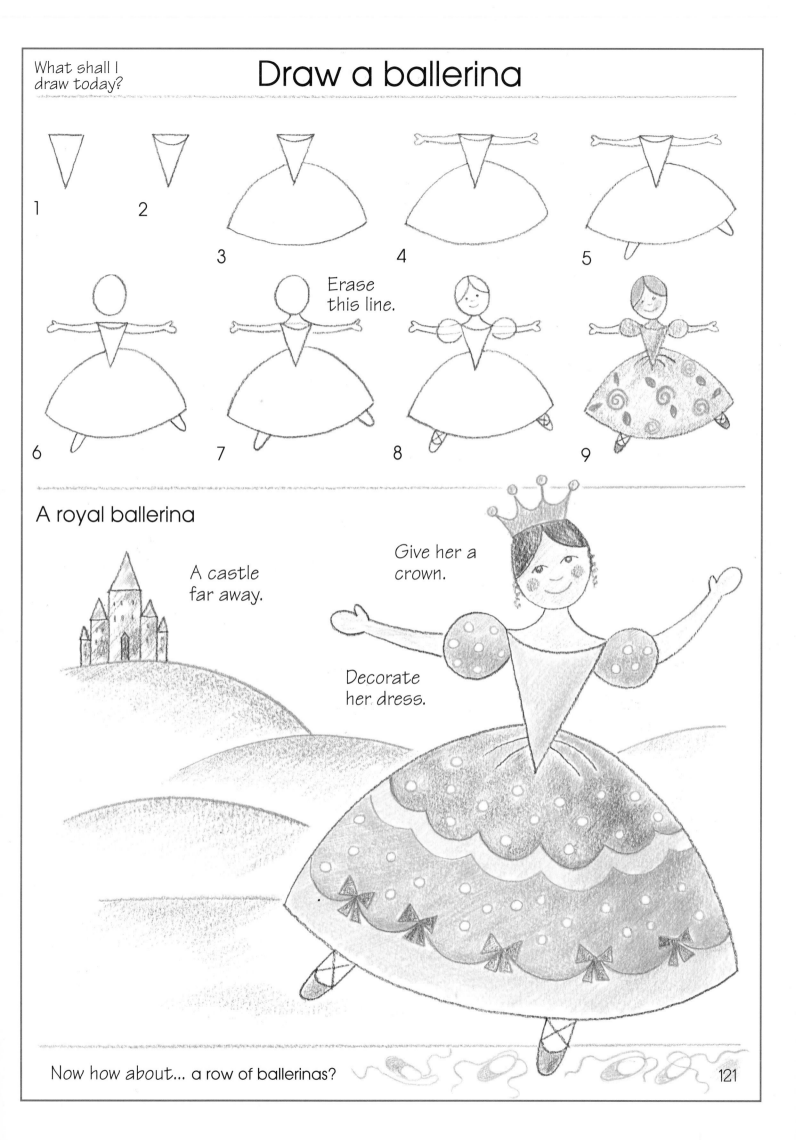

1

2

3

4

5

Erase this line.

6

7

8

9

A royal ballerina

A castle far away.

Give her a crown.

Decorate her dress.

Draw a teddy

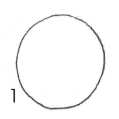 1

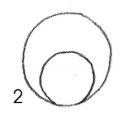 2

 3

 4

 5

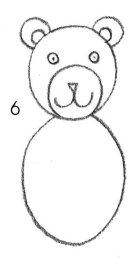 6

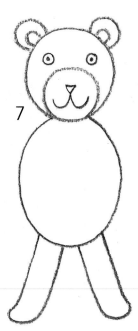 7

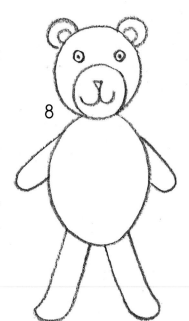 8

 9

Walking Teddy

Erase the lines you don't need.

Sitting teddy

Erase the lines you don't need.

Shouting teddy

Draw the mouth open.

Teddy
bears'
picnic

Teddies
playing

Shading
for
straight
fur

Squiggles
for curly
fur

Now how about... teddy bears at a swimming pool?

Draw a castle

Leave gaps here

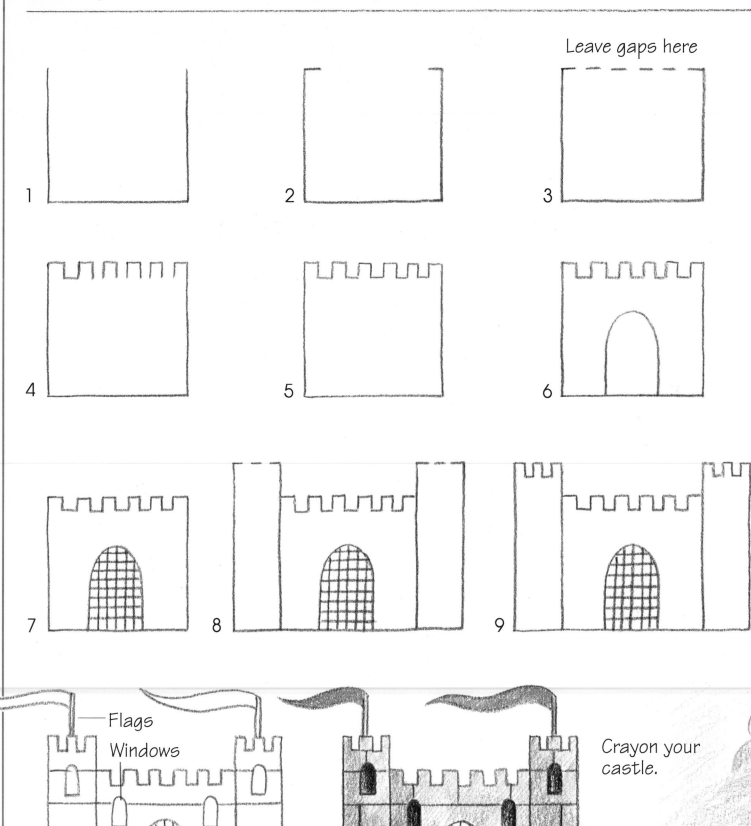

1

2

3

4

5

6

7

8

9

Flags

Windows

10

Draw lines going across.

11

Add lines going down.

Crayon your
castle.

A castle on fire

Red and
orange flames

Add clouds
of smoke.

Make all the flames
go the same way.

Wiggly blue lines
for the castle moat

Buckets of water

Now how about... a castle in a storm with lightning?

Draw a pick-up truck

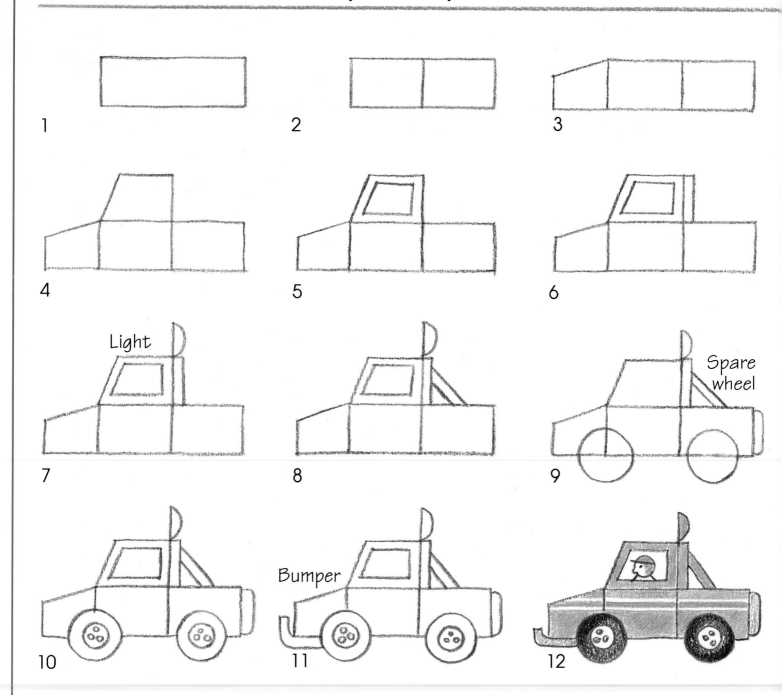

1

2

3

4

5

6

7 Light

8

9 Spare wheel

10

11 Bumper

12

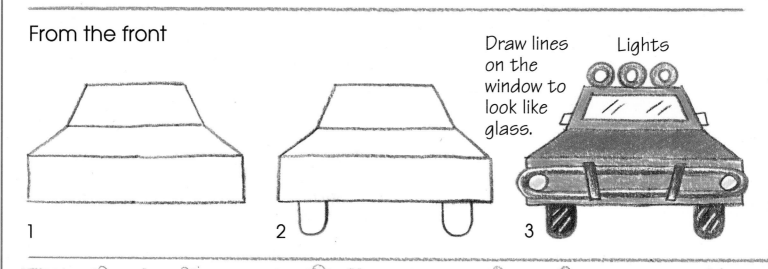

From the front

1

2

3 Draw lines on the window to look like glass. Lights

Draw a car

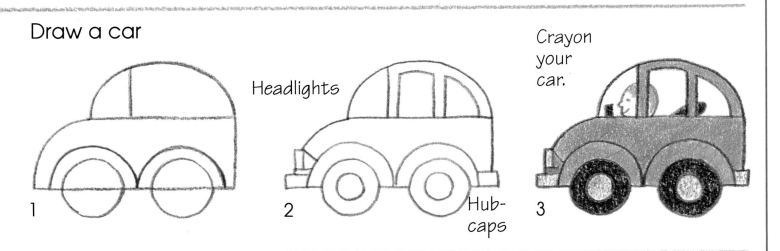

Headlights

Crayon your car.

Hub-caps

1   2   3

Pick up trucks at work

Draw a pick-up truck pulling a car out of a lake.

Add scenery

Pick-up trucks can go up steep slopes.

Now how about... a pick-up truck rescuing a racing car?

Things to do with your drawings

Mounting

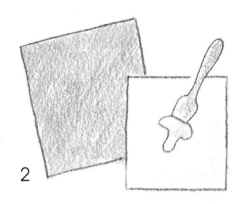

1

Take a piece of paper or cardboard, a little bigger than your drawing.

2

Spread glue thinly over the back of the drawing. Put it in the middle of the mount.

3

With clean hands, smooth your drawing down firmly.

Fancy mounts

Decorate your mount with wrapping paper.

Cut a wiggly edge for your mount with scissors.

Draw a simple pattern on your mount.

Sprinkle glitter on your mount or stick on shiny stars.

Making a shaped card

Fold a piece of cardboard in half. Stick your drawing close to the fold. Leaving the folded side, cut around your drawing, close to the edge.

What shall I paint?

Contents

What shall I paint today?

Paint a parrot

1. Paint the body, like this.

2. Make a hand print on either side for the wings.

3. Paint the tail. Add wingtips.

4. Paint the head.

5. Add a beak, eye and claws.

6. Add tips to the wings and tail.

To paint a perching parrot, make a hand print on a slant.

Then paint the rest of the parrot as before.

130 - Now how about... a row of perching parrots on a long branch?

To print a leafy background, paint the rough side of a leaf and press it onto the paper.

131

Paint a cat on a rug

1. Draw a cat's head in crayon near one side of your sheet of paper.

2. Now draw its body. Add a face, tail and whiskers. Go over the lines again.

3. With a new crayon, draw a big oblong around the cat. Add stripes and patterns.

4. Now paint over the cat, using runny black paint. The cat will show through.

5. Paint the rug area in different shades. The patterns will show through.

6. Crayon a fringe at both ends of your rug to finish off the picture.

You could use only one shade of paint for the rug.

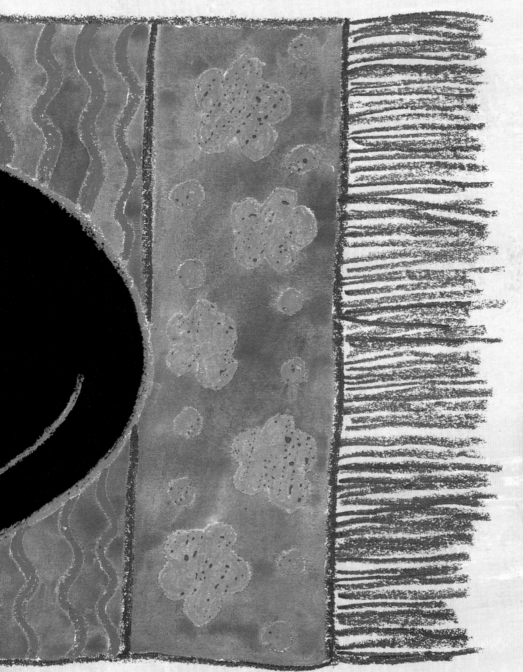

A cat in the grass

Draw a cat with a yellow crayon. Crayon flowers around it. Paint over the cat with orange paint and over the flowers with green paint.

   Now how about... a window with patterned curtains?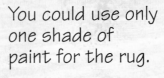

Paint a monster

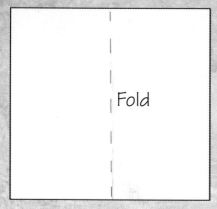

1. Fold your paper in half. Press down firmly and then open it.

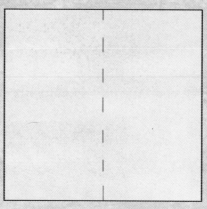

2. With a damp cloth, wipe on some blue paint for the sky.

3. Paint a tree shape down one side. Fold your paper again and press down firmly.

4. When you open it, there will be trees down both edges of the paper. Allow to dry.

5. Paint some blobs near the middle of the paper like this. Use monster-ish shades.

6. Fold and press the paper again. Open it out. When the paint is dry, add eyes and teeth.

Now how about... an alien?

Paint a scary picture

Haunted woods

 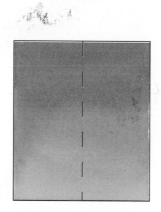  

1. Fold your paper in half. Press down firmly, then open it out again.

2. With a damp cloth, wipe on some red and yellow paint.

3. Paint trees on one side with runny black paint. Fold and press.

4. When dry, paint scary eyes among your spooky trees.

A dragon

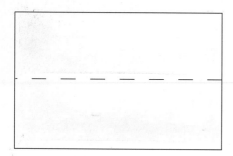 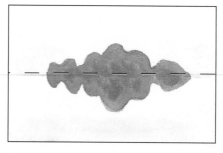 

1. Fold your paper in half, press down firmly and open it out again.

2. Paint some blobs near the middle. Fold and press, then open the paper.

3. Paint the head, legs and tail when dry.

Eyes

Teeth

Now how about... a shaggy dog?

Paint penguins on the ice

Ice

Sea

Icy sea

1. With a damp cloth, wipe white paint over one end of the paper.

2. In the same way, wipe blue paint over the rest of it.

3. Paint some clingwrap white. Press the painted side over the blue.

4. Lift it off gently and repeat until all the blue is patterned with white.

Penguins

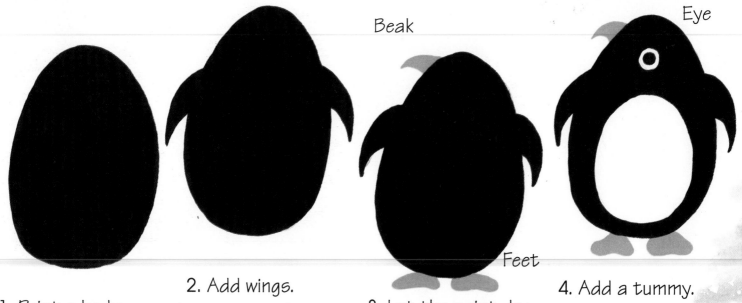

Beak

Eye

Feet

1. Paint a body.

2. Add wings.

3. Let the paint dry.

4. Add a tummy.

Fish

1.

2.

3.

138

Now how about... ducks on a frozen pond?

Paint flowers

Poppies

1. Make some swirly petal shapes with a pale candle.

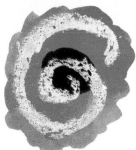

2. Paint over them like this.

Daisies

1. Draw loopy petal shapes with the candle.

2. Paint over them like this.

Tulips

1. Draw upright petal shapes with the candle.

2. Paint over them like this.

Buds

1. Draw small squiggles with the candle.

2. Paint over them like this.

Now how about... a big hat with flowers on it?

Paint a truck

1. Take an oblong sponge and dip the end in paint. Press it onto your paper.

2. Carefully print two more oblongs on either side of the first one.

3. For the engine, print a fourth oblong on its side in front of the first three.

Paint a busy road

Now try painting lots of trucks, vans and buses.

Use the big side of your sponge to print this van.

For the bus, use the long, narrow side of the sponge.

This small truck has three wheels.

You could add some road signs to your picture.

4. For the driver's cab, dip the end of a matchbox in paint and print two lines.

5. Use a round, cut potato to print wheels. Print a headlight using the end of a cork.

6. To make the road, dip crumpled paper in grey paint and press it along the paper under your truck.

It's fun to make up signs of your own.

Print windows with the end of a matchbox.

Use a matchbox to print the three oblongs on the front.

Paint a bonfire

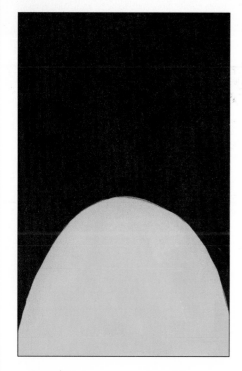

1. Take a piece of black paper and some runny yellow paint. Paint a bonfire shape.

2. Using runny red paint, add some wiggly stripes to your bonfire shape.

3. Using your fingers, mix the paint together to make flames.

4. Crumple up some paper and dip it in white paint. Dab it on for the smoke.

5. Paint black sticks and logs. Don't worry if the paints mix.

6. Splash on some big sparks with your paintbrush. It's best to do this outside.

Now how about... a firework display?

Paint a cactus in the desert

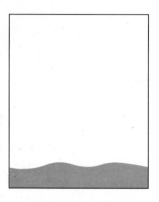

1. Paint a wiggly line for sand at the bottom of very large paper.

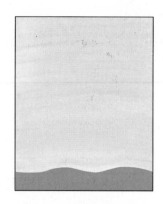

2. With a damp cloth, wipe on some paint for the sky.

3. In the same way wipe on some red streaks for clouds.

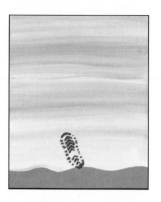

4. Paint the bottom of a clean rubber shoe or boot. Press it onto your paper.

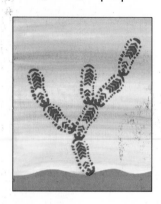

5. Make more overlapping shoe prints. Repaint the shoe each time.

6. Add pink flowers and a bright sun with a paintbrush.

7. Dip your fingers in orange paint and print some stones.

Cactus

Birds

Flowers

In the desert, some cacti grow taller than people.

Stones

Paint a sky picture

1. Cut cloud shapes
out of scrap paper.
Lay them on a large
sheet of thick paper.

2. With a damp sponge,
gently dab blue paint
around the edges of all
your clouds.

3. When the whole
sheet of paper is
covered with blue, peel
the clouds off gently.

4. Paint some hot air
balloons in the sky.
Add some planes
doing exciting stunts.

5. When the planes
and balloons have
dried, decorate them
with bright patterns.

6. Add smoke trails to
the planes using a
piece of damp sponge
dipped in paint.

Now how about... kites in the sky?

Paint sheep in a field

3. Wind some yarn or wool around an old birthday card. You don't need to wind it very neatly. When the card is covered, tape down the end and cut off the leftover yarn.

1. Draw sheep's bodies and lambs' bodies on pieces of scrap paper. Cut them out.

2. Dip them in water. Shake off the drops, then arrange them on your painting paper.

150

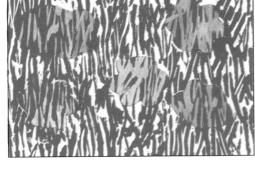

4. Paint the yarn green on one side. Press it all over your paper. Add more paint as you go.

5. Gently peel off the paper sheep. Paint on faces and legs with a fine paintbrush.

6. Add some flowers. Print them with a fingertip.

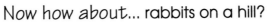

Paint a face

1. Ask a grown-up to cut a big potato in half.

2. Dip the cut half of the potato in some paint. Print a face with it.

3. Mix some runny paint. Pour some along the top of your printed face.

4. For hair, blow through a straw onto the paint.

5. Print the eyes with a finger dipped in paint.

Add long hair and a crown for a princess.

6. Paint the nose and the mouth.

Add ears that stick out and a round mouth for a baby.

Now how about... some animals, using potato prints for the bodies?

For a clown, add bright hair, a red nose and a hat.

You could add a tangly beard as well as hair.

Try adding funny glasses or a bow tie.

153

Paint a scarecrow

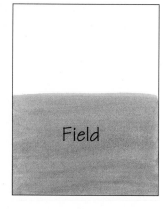

1. Dip a damp cloth in brown paint. Wipe it over about half your paper.

2. Still using a damp cloth wipe blue paint over the rest of your paper.

3. With a clean damp cloth blot some of the blue paint off again.

4. Thicken yellow paint with some flour. Finger-paint rows of corn.

5. With thick paint, finger-paint a turnip-shaped head. Add a stick body.

6. Now finger-paint some clothes. Add eyes and a mouth and a carrot nose.

7. Dip the edge of some cardboard in yellow paint. Print some straw hair.

Paint pigs in some straw

Paint some pigs. You could use your fingers or a paint brush.

Print the straw with the edge of some cardboard.

Now how about... some birds in a nest?

Paint fish in a waterfall

1. With a damp cloth, wipe blue stripes down your paper.

2. Add some green stripes to your paper in the same way.

3. Make white handprints along the bottom of your paper.

4. Splash some white paint on with a brush to look like spray.

5. On another piece of paper paint lots of bright fish.

6. Let the paint dry. Add patterns on top.

7. Cut the fish out. Glue them onto the waterfall picture.

Now how about... an underwater picture with handprints for seaweed?

Paint a pattern

1. Mix flour with two
different shades of
paint to make it
really thick.

2. Cut an old
postcard in half.
Cut V shapes all
along one of the
shorter edges.

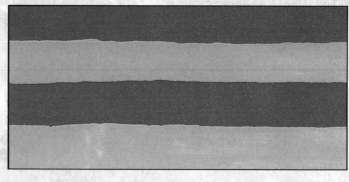

3. Take a big sheet of thick paper. Paint
some thick stripes on it using two shades.

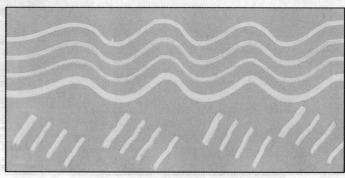

4. Scrape lots of different patterns into
the painted stripes using the straight
end of the card.

5. Then scrape patterns into the stripes
using the zig zag end of the card. Make
some straight and some wavy.

Butterfly

1. Paint thickly over a big sheet of paper.

3. Use a pencil to draw half a butterfly shape against the fold. Trace over the shape with your finger, pressing hard.

2. Fold in half, painted side in.

4. Open it out.

To change a pattern, paint over it and start again.

Paint more patterns

1. Fold a sheet of kitchen towel in half and in half again.

2. Fold it in half twice more, pressing hard.

3. Dip the corners into runny paint.

4. Put the folded kitchen towel between some sheets of newspaper. Roll over hard, with a rolling pin.

5. Take out the kitchen towel and open it very gently.

Other shapes

Fold a piece of towel into a triangle and dip the sides or the corners.

Fold a piece of towel into a rectangle and dip each side of it in paint.

What shall I make?

Contents

Make a talking bird

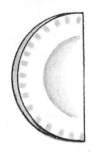  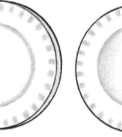  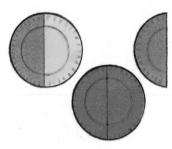 

You don't need these.

1. Fold three paper plates in half. Then, bend each one back along the fold.

2. Cut one plate along the fold. Cut a strip from the edge of one half.

3. Mix household glue (PVA) with red, orange and yellow paint. Paint the plates like this.

4. When the paint has dried, put the two whole plates together like this.

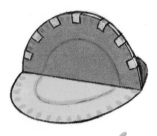 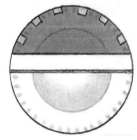

5. Tape the orange and red parts together around the edge.

6. Turn it over and tape the orange piece onto the red half.

7. Make a roll of crêpe paper. Cut lots of slits in it.

8. Tape the paper onto the back of the yellow part.

9. Glue on paper eyes. You could glue on buttons for the middles.

You could add bright feathers instead of paper to the bird's head.

10. Cut a hole in a sock for your thumb and put your hand inside.

11. Put your hand into the bird. Open and close your hand to make it talk.

163

Make a wobbling head

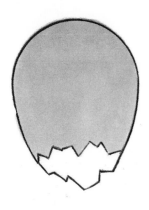

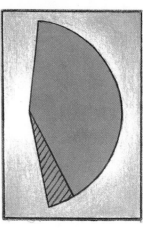

1. Paint a clean eggshell. Dry it upside down. Roll a ball of model dough the size of a marble.

2. Wet a finger and rub it on one side of the model dough. Press it into the bottom of the egg.

3. Cut lots of pieces of yarn for hair. Glue them around the top of the eggshell.

4. Put tracing paper over the pattern for the hat on page 192. Draw over the lines carefully.

Sprinkle glitter onto dots of glue.

Add a pair of glasses and a gift wrap hat.

 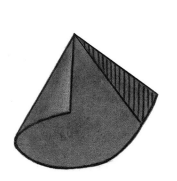  

5. Glue the tracing paper onto bright paper with a glue stick. Cut around the shape.

6. Put glue on the shaded part of the pattern. Overlap the sides. Press them together.

7. Glue around the inside edge of the hat. Push the hat over the hair onto the head.

8. Paint a nose and a smiling mouth. Add middles to the eyes in a different shade.

Add lots of shapes all over the hat.

Cut a crown from shiny paper.

Make a parachute

1. Cut one side from a plastic carrier bag. Lay it flat.

2. Lay this book on top. Draw around it with a pen.

3. Cut it out. Fold over the top corner like this. Draw a line.

4. Fold the corner back up and cut along the line.

5. Poke a hole in each corner with a ballpoint pen.

6. Cut four pieces of thread as long as this book.

7. Poke one piece through one of the holes. Tie a knot.

8. Do the same with the other three corners.

9. Bring all the ends together. Tie them in a big knot.

10. Tape the knot to the back of a small model.

Fly your
parachute
outside. Crumple
it in your hand.
Put the model on
top and throw them
high into the air.

167

Make a furry snake

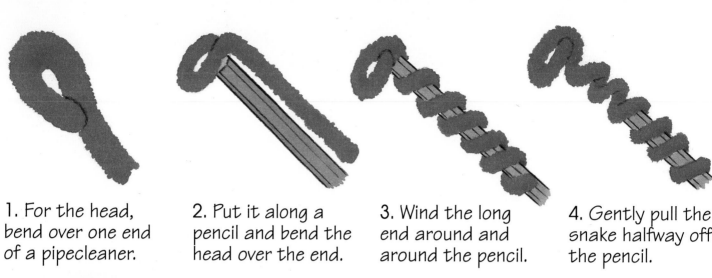

1. For the head, bend over one end of a pipecleaner.

2. Put it along a pencil and bend the head over the end.

3. Wind the long end around and around the pencil.

4. Gently pull the snake halfway off the pencil.

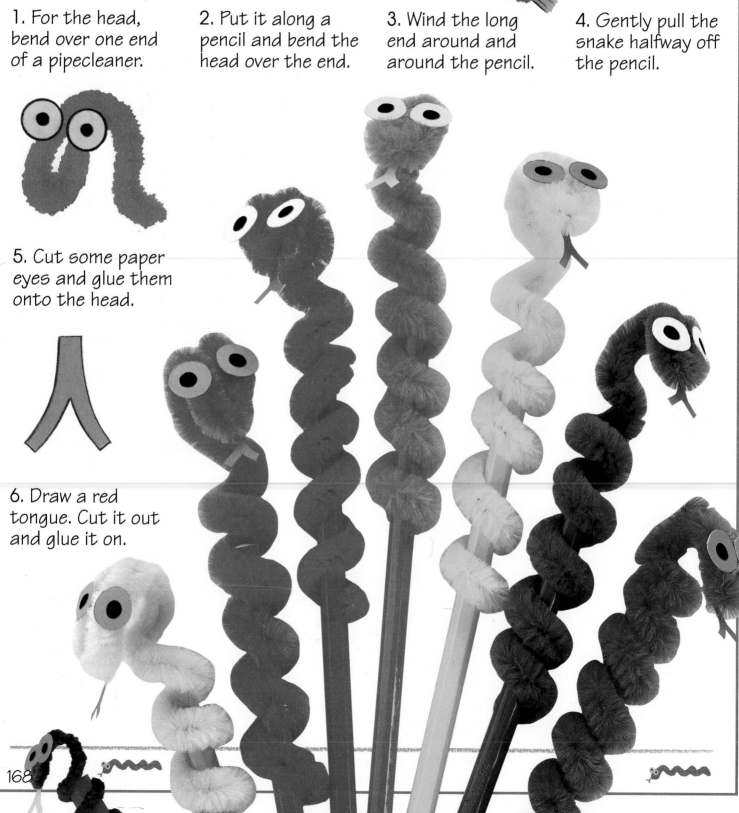

5. Cut some paper eyes and glue them onto the head.

6. Draw a red tongue. Cut it out and glue it on.

Make some bangles

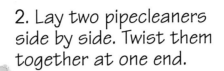

1. Take two pencils and tape them together like this.

2. Lay two pipecleaners side by side. Twist them together at one end.

3. Put the pencils between the pipecleaners, close to the twisted part.

4. Twist the pipecleaners tightly next to the pencils, three times.

5. Pull out the pencils. Put them in between the pipecleaners and twist.

6. Keep on doing this to the end. Press the twisted pipecleaners flat.

7. Bend them into a circle. Twist the ends together.

Make a mask

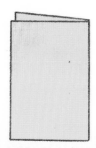  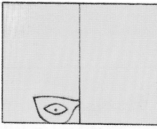 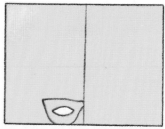

1. Take some stiff paper as big as this book. Fold it in half, short sides together.

2. Put some sunglasses along the bottom, halfway across the fold.

3. Draw around the shape. Add an eye, then poke a hole in it with a pencil.

4. Push scissors into the hole. Cut to the edge of the eye, then cut it out.

Glue on shiny shapes and sequins.

5. Fold the paper again. Draw around the eye shape onto the paper below.

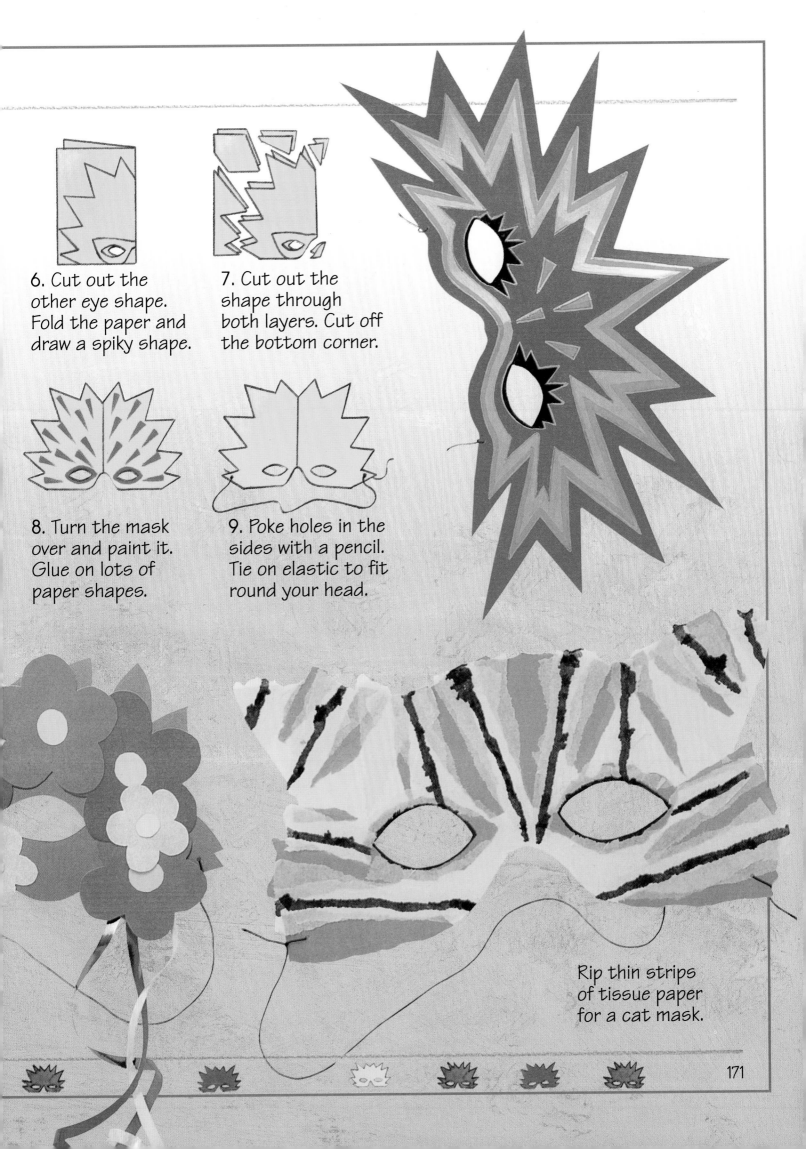

6. Cut out the other eye shape. Fold the paper and draw a spiky shape.

7. Cut out the shape through both layers. Cut off the bottom corner.

8. Turn the mask over and paint it. Glue on lots of paper shapes.

9. Poke holes in the sides with a pencil. Tie on elastic to fit round your head.

Rip thin strips of tissue paper for a cat mask.

Make some vegetable people

1. Wash and dry a large potato. Cut a slice off one end so that it stands up.

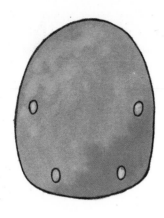

2. Poke four holes in the front of the potato with a sharp pencil.

3. Cut two pipecleaners in half. Push a piece into each hole.

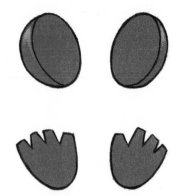

4. Make hands and feet from small balls of model dough.

5. Press the hands and feet onto the ends of the pipecleaners.

6. Make a face by adding a round nose and a smiling mouth.

7. Press on two circles for eyes. Add smaller middles to them.

8. Press model dough through a sieve and scrape it off with a knife. Press it on.

A flower hat

Ball of model dough

Strip of model dough

Flat model dough

Push the ball onto the flat piece. Roll up lots of strips to make flowers. Press them on.

A tall hat

Roll of model dough

Circle of model dough

Add a band.

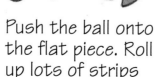

A bag

Squashed ball of model dough

Add a handle.

Add a clip.

You can make
people from
all types of
vegetables.

Make bread shapes

These bread shapes are decorations only. Do not eat them.

1. Press a big cookie cutter firmly into a slice of white bread.

2. Push the shape gently out of the cutter.

3. Make a hole by pressing the end of a straw into the shape.

4. Put it onto a baking rack and leave it overnight to go hard.

5. Mix a little paint with household glue (PVA). Paint the edges of the shape.

6. Paint the top. When it is dry, turn it over and paint the other side.

174

7. Glue on lots of glitter, sequins or beads to decorate your shape.

8. Push thread through the hole. Bring the ends together to make a loop.

9. Push the ends of the thread through the loop to make a knot.

Make paper flowers

A daisy

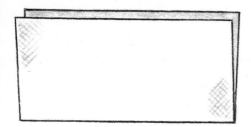  

1. Fold a sheet of kitchen paper towel in half. Open it out. Cut along the fold.

2. Fold one piece in half, long sides together. You don't need the other piece.

3. Draw lots of stripes along the paper with a felt-tip pen.

   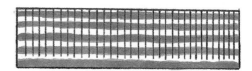

4. Fold in half with the short sides together, then fold it in half again.

5. Make long cuts close together from the bottom. Don't cut all the way up.

6. Open it carefully, so that it looks like this.

7. Tape one end of the paper onto a bendable straw. Roll the paper tightly around it.

8. Fasten the loose end with tape. Pull all the petals down.

9. Snip little pieces of yellow paper or yarn. Glue them into the middle.

You can use tissue paper for bright flowers. Cut the paper the same size as a piece of paper towel.

Another flower

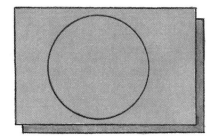

1. Take two sheets of tissue paper. Put a small plate or saucer on top and draw around it.

2. Cut around the circle through both layers of tissue paper. Fold them in half and in half again.

3. Twist the corner and tape onto the end of a straw. Gently pull the petals apart.

4. Make a ball of tissue paper and glue it in the middle.

Make a fish

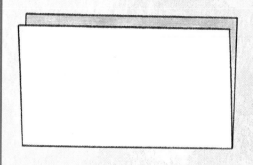

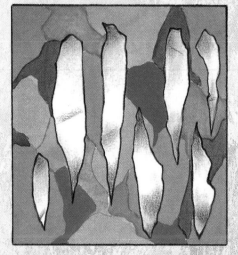

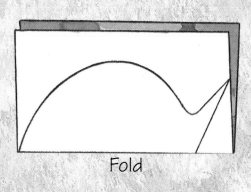

Fold

1. Fold a piece of paper in half, long sides together. Open it. Crease it back along the same fold.

2. Open the paper. Tear pieces of tissue paper. Glue them on. Add lots of strips of kitchen foil.

3. Fold the paper in half. Crease the fold well. Draw half a fat fish shape. Cut it out.

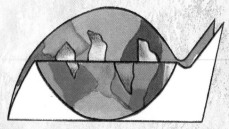

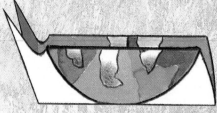

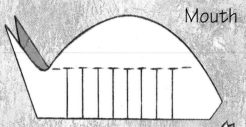

Mouth

4. Bend over one of the top edges until it touches the fold at the bottom. Press hard to crease it.

5. Turn the fish over. Bend the other top edge over in the same way. Remember to crease it well.

6. Unfold the top pieces. Snip a mouth. Make cuts as wide as your finger, up to the fold.

7. Half open the fish. Hold the head and pull the first strip out. Pinch the fold in the middle so that it stands up.

8. Skip the next strip. Pull out the next one. Go on in the same way until you reach the last strip. Pinch all the folds well.

Use bright
thread to
hang up
your fish.

Make model dough babies

 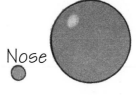  

1. Make a ball of pink and yellow model dough, the size shown here. Roll them together.

2. Break off a tiny piece and roll the rest back into a ball. Press on the nose.

3. Press in eyes with a pencil. Press a mouth with the end of a straw.

4. Make a ball this size. Use a round pencil like a rolling pin to make it flat.

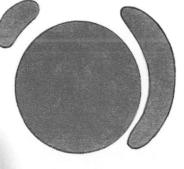  

5. Turn a mug upside down and press it on. Peel away the spare model dough

6. Press a pencil point around the edge to make it lacy. Turn it over.

7. Put the head near the top. Press on a sausage shape for the body.

8. Wrap one side around the body, then wrap the other side over the top.

9. Gently press the blanket around the baby's head and neck.

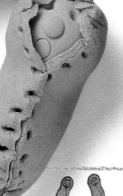 

Nose

Make an octopus

1. Roll a model dough sausage. Flatten it. Roll balls for eyes and press them on.

2. Push a pencil point into each eye. Make a mouth with the end of a spoon.

3. Use scissors to snip eight tentacles. Bend up the side ones.

4. Press the end of a straw into the legs, to make lots of suckers.

5. Make seaweed from strips of green model dough. Cut out some fish.

Make a row of clowns

1. Put tracing paper over the clown pattern on page 192. Draw over the black lines.

2. Draw around all the red lines with a red pencil. Take the paper off.

3. Carefully cut around the black lines, but don't cut out the clown.

4. Glue the tracing onto the corner of a long sheet of stiff paper.

5. Turn the paper over. Fold the clown to the front. Crease along the edge.

6. Turn the paper over again. Neatly fold the clown back to the front.

7. Turn it over. Fold it to the front again. Cut off the extra paper at the top and side.

8. Cut out the clown along the red lines. Don't cut the black lines at the edges.

9. Pull the clowns open, so that the tracing is on the back. Draw their hats.

10. Draw the clowns' faces. Use paint or felt-tip pens to decorate their clothes.

Make a crown

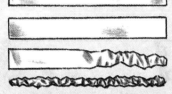

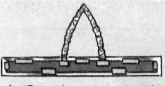

1. Cut a band of stiff paper to fit around your head, plus a little bit.

2. Lay it on a bigger piece of kitchen foil. Fold the edges in and tape them down.

3. Cut four strips of foil as wide as the band. Squeeze them to make thin sticks.

4. Bend one in half. Tape it onto the middle of the band, at the back.

5. Cut a little from the end of two pieces. Bend them and tape them on.

6. Cut the last piece in half. Bend each piece. Tape them on at each end.

7. Cut shiny shapes. Tape them on so you can see them above the band.

8. Turn the band over. Glue on scraps of bright paper or foil.

For an icy crown, use only blue and silver paper.

Make a smaller crown for a ballerina.

9. Tape the ends of the crown together to fit around your head.

For a king's crown, add shapes cut from shiny paper. Add spots with a felt-tip pen for a fur effect.

185

Make a lacy card

1. Draw some leaves, flowers and hearts on thick white paper.

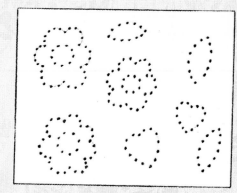

2. Wrap sticky tape around the end of a darning needle to make a handle. Lay several kitchen paper towels over a folded newspaper. Put your drawing on top.

3. Use the needle to prick around the shapes. Press quite hard.

4. Cut around all the shapes very carefully. Leave a narrow edge around the holes.

5. Dab glue stick on the pencil side of each shape. Press them very gently onto thin cardboard.

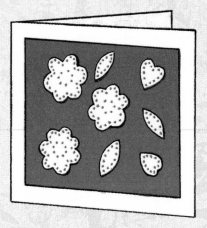

6. To make a card, glue your picture onto a slightly bigger piece of folded cardboard.

Make stamps

Draw a stamp and prick around the edges. Tear it carefully along the holes.

You don't need to use white paper for all your shapes.

Prick a wavy line around your shape Cut around it, but leave a narrow edge.

187

Make a caterpillar

1. Put this book onto a piece of bright paper. Draw around it and cut it out.

2. Fold it in half. Cut along the fold. Sponge different paint on both sides of one piece.

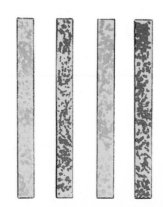

3. Fold the paper in half and in half again. Open it and cut along all the folds.

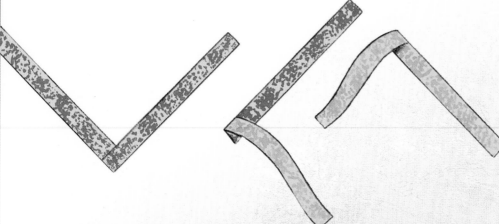

4. Put some glue at the end of one strip and join it to another one like this.

5. Fold the left strip over and crease it. Fold the other strip down over it.

6. Keep folding one strip over the other one to make a concertina shape.

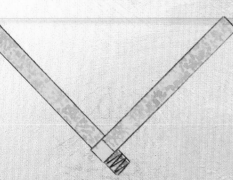

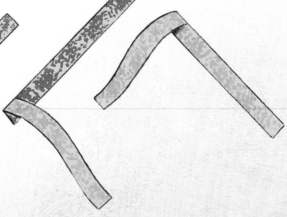

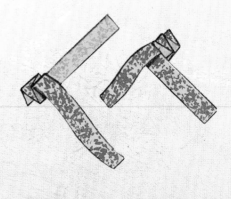

7. When you get near to the end of the strips, glue on the spare strips, then keep on folding.

8. When you reach the end glue down the top piece. Trim the ends. Add eyes, feelers and a tail.

9. Tape some thin elastic behind the head and the tail. Tie the caterpillar onto a straw.

Make a brooch

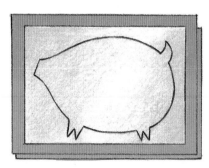

1. Put tracing paper over the pig pattern on page 192. Draw around the shape.

2. Put two pieces of felt together. Pin the tracing paper pattern on top.

3. Cut around the shape. Ask for help for the tricky parts. Take out the pins.

4. Cut the tail from one pig. Trace the pig's ear on page 192. Cut one out from felt.

5. Pin the pigs together. Sew around them with big stitches. Take out the pins.

6. Now sew close to the edge with tiny stitches. Leave a gap at the bottom.

Draw stripes on with a pen.

Glue sequins and beads onto your brooch.

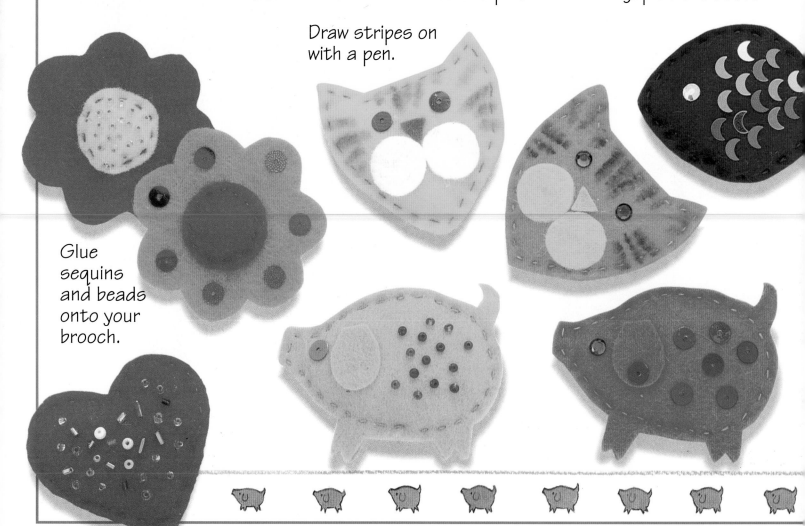

7. Take out the big stitches. Carefully push some stuffing into the hole.

8. Sew up the hole. Glue on the ear. Draw an eye with a felt-tip pen.

9. Turn the pig over. Sew a safety pin onto the back of the brooch.

The patterns for the other brooches shown here are on page 192.

Patterns

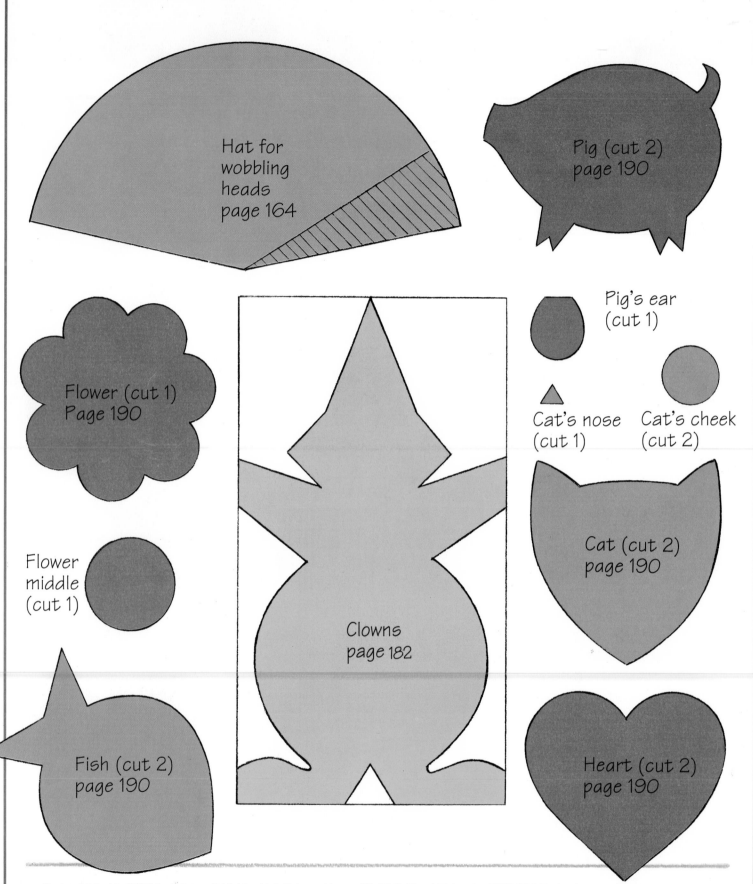

Hat for wobbling heads page 164

Pig (cut 2) page 190

Pig's ear (cut 1)

Cat's nose (cut 1)

Cat's cheek (cut 2)

Flower (cut 1) Page 190

Flower middle (cut 1)

Clowns page 182

Cat (cut 2) page 190

Fish (cut 2) page 190

Heart (cut 2) page 190

First published in 2003 by Usborne Publishing Ltd., Usborne House, 83-85 Saffron Hill, London EC1N 8RT, England. www.usborne.com. Copyright © 2003, 1997, 1996, 1995, 1994 Usborne Publishing Ltd. The name Usborne and the device ♀ ⊕ are Trade Marks of Usborne Publishing Ltd. All rights reserved. No part of this publication may be reproduced, stored in a retrieval system, or transmitted in any form or by any means, electronic, mechanical, photocopying, recording or otherwise without the prior permission of the publisher. AE. First published in America 2003. Printed in Italy.